EMBRACING GOD'S WORLD

Also by Joyce Huggett:

Encountering God

Finding Freedom

Listening to God

Listening to Others

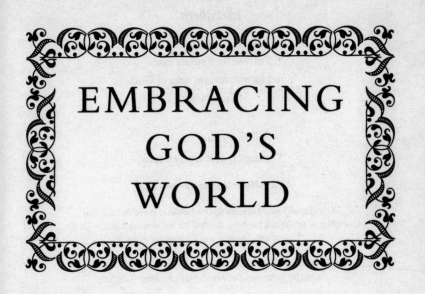

EMBRACING
GOD'S
WORLD

Joyce Huggett

Hodder & Stoughton
LONDON SYDNEY AUCKLAND

For
Elizabeth

God is a loving potter.
You are his treasure rare.
You bear the fingermarks of God.
Thank you.

Copyright © 1996 Joyce Huggett

First published in Great Britain 1996.

The right of Joyce Huggett to be identified as the Author and
Compiler of the Work has been asserted by her in accordance with the
Copyright, Designs and Patents Act 1988.

Scripture quotations from *The Message*, copyright © 1993, 1994, 1995,
used by permission of NavPress Publishing Group.

While every effort has been made to contact the copyright holders of
prayers used in this book, this has not always been successful.
Full acknowledgment will gladly be made in future editions.

10 9 8 7 6 5 4 3 2 1

British Library Cataloguing in Publication Data:
A record for this book is available from the British Library.

ISBN 0 340 65620 4

Typeset in Monotype Bembo by Strathmore Publishing Services, London N7.
Printed and bound in Great Britain by Cox & Wyman Ltd, Reading, Berkshire.

Hodder and Stoughton Ltd,
A division of Hodder Headline PLC
338 Euston Road, London NW1 3BH

Contents

Acknowledgments

When I agreed to collate this book of prayers, I never imagined that the project would bring so many new friends into my life. Corresponding with the authors of some of the prayers I have quoted has been a humbling and enriching experience and I now feel as though my circle of friends has widened considerably. I want to put on record my indebtedness to friends old and new for their help in putting this book together. To write a prayer is to reveal an intimate part of oneself – that hidden part we normally share only with God. To have a prayer published is to share with the world one's spiritual secrets. Yet, when I have asked former strangers as well as familiar friends for permission to reveal their secret selves by printing their prayers, they have been more than generous in their replies. For this and for the richness and warmth of the correspondence that has been generated, I shall always be grateful.

As always, I owe a debt of gratitude, too, to my prayer supporters who prayed this book into being. Without them, I would certainly not have met my deadline. Because of their backing and the great grace of God, inspiration flowed and energised me – even when I was battling with a debilitating virus.

My husband, David, and James Catford of Hodder and Stoughton are both great encouragers. I drew strength from their support and am grateful for them both. I am indebted too, to Pauline Gallagher for the practical help she gave me at the proof-reading stage.

I have personally been very moved when typing up some of these prayers. Behind them lies a wealth of experience, often of untold suffering and always, of self-dedication. I count it a great privilege to spread before my readers the expressions of commitment of so many of God's unsung heroes and heroines. As the book goes to print, I pray that users of it will find themselves consistently wooed into a deeper relationship with the God it exalts; that they will find themselves compelled to embrace God's wonderful, needy world.

Joyce Huggett, Cyprus, 1996

Introduction

> Compassionate caring is the acid test of the authentic Christ-following life ...
> the Christlike person formed gradually by the Spirit will be characterised by
> an ever-growing responsiveness and sensitivity to the pain of others ...
> Compassion, in the way of Jesus, places our lives beside those in turmoil,
> seeks understanding of their anguish and labours with them for the sake of
> their greater wholeness.[1]

Over the years, those far-reaching claims have been woven into the
very fibre of my being. The process began in a life-changing way
shortly after the publication of *Listening to God*. That book describes
how I found myself being drawn into the, for me, previously unex-
plored worlds of contemplative prayer and charismatic prayer. To mark
the publication of the book, BBC Radio Nottingham broadcast an
interview with me during which Jeremy, the interviewer, invited me to
tell more of my story. After the interview, while Jeremy and I sat chat-
ting over a cup of coffee,he asked his most dynamic question: 'Joyce!
I'm interested that there's no reference to social justice in *Listening to
God*. Yet surely, prayer and social justice go together? Maybe that'll be
the subject of your next book?'

The subject of my next book was not social justice though it was
about compassion for others. Several years were to elapse before I was
to write with conviction: 'The closer we come to the compassionate
Christ, the more we will catch his compassion for his world – particu-
larly the world of the poor and the marginalised.' And several more
years were to elapse before I was to hear and respond to God's call to
leave the comparative comfort of the small corner of the world with
which I was familiar and to give my consent to being catapulted into the
great unknown of living and working overseas. The Holy Spirit shapes
and re-shapes us sensitively and slowly, at a pace we can cope with. He
knew when the time was ripe for me to embrace God's world in a new
way.

One of the ways in which he jolted me out of my Christian compla-
cency into an awareness that he wanted to send me to far-flung corners
of the world was through a meditation popularised by St Ignatius. In
this meditation, we are invited to step back in time to the pre-Christian

era: those days before the birth of Christ when the voice of God seemed strangely silent. We are invited, too, to imagine ourselves sitting in the heavenly places with the Holy Trinity: the Father, the Son and the Holy Spirit. As the three members of the Holy Trinity look down on a world hurtling to destruction, we gaze at the world also. As I recorded in my journal at the time:

I found it awesome to sit with the Father, the Son and the Holy Spirit and to take a peep at today's world:

Tanzania where children beg for pencils so that they can attend school. Kenya where the standard of living is comparatively high and yet pathetically low compared to the West. Poland where Christians still struggle to survive. Eastern Europe where thousands are turning to Christ but where children are born with AIDS and where most people live below the poverty line. The town where I live, where good, generous people live alongside drunkards, those who over-eat, those who exploit girls from the East, those who are greedy for gain.

As now, so then. The world hurtled to disaster.

The Holy Trinity did not remain unmoved. The moment had clearly come to put Operation Rescue into motion. So the Angel Gabriel was sent to the little town of Nazareth to invite Mary to become the mother of the Messiah. Mary: a woman dear to God's heart, 'blessed among women', not because she could boast rank or reputation, but because she was as soft clay in the Creator's hands. Her heart had already been turned to her Saviour. Mary who, by her ready yes and by God's grace, made possible the impossible. Mary who, now pregnant with Christ, carried the Saviour of the world wherever she went: to family and friends, to the village well or the bazaar on the hillside.

As I pondered these mysteries, God seemed to read my struggles and speak into them. I wanted to be like Mary: ready to say 'yes' to whatever God would ask of me. The week before, I had re-dedicated my life to God and his service. But to be like Mary! Was such readiness possible? My mind focused only on those treasures I might be asked to renounce: family, friends, the familiarity of home, country and culture.

'Nothing is impossible with me,' God implored. 'You don't have to renounce anything, but rather receive Someone. The Holy Spirit will come upon you and overshadow you as he overshadowed Mary.'

'Mary was not asked to renounce anything but to receive an incredible gift. God longs to impregnate us with his divine energy and power,' I wrote in my journal. I was on a five-week retreat at the time. By the end of the retreat, I had, indeed, been overshadowed afresh by God's life-changing Spirit. He had injected into me a passion for the world which is but a pale reflection of the Holy Trinity's passion for the universe and its people.

Now, embracing God's world is a passion. That is why, when James Catford of Hodder and Stoughton invited me to collate this book of prayers, I chose *Embracing God's World* as the title. The title was inspired by a small booklet entitled *Embrace the World* by Mary Euphrasia that I had stumbled on while I was on another retreat in Singapore. The booklet contains sayings penned by a woman of God whose passion for the world prompted her to write prayers like this:

> O Jesus,
> you are my life,
> my Beloved,
> my all.
> I offer you my life,
> I give you my heart,
> I wish what you wish,
> nothing but your holy will.

> – *Mary Euphrasia Pelletier* [2]

and exhortations and reflections like these: 'Courage! How many persons will owe their lives to your sacrifices?',[3] 'Remember all your strength comes from God',[4] 'O! How beautiful is the prayer of a person who in silence listens to God's voice',[5] 'Only in solitude and silence can God's voice be heard in our hearts'[6] (see also page 14).

I use that booklet daily. When I am weary, the exhortations encourage me in the sense that they pour courage into me. When I find myself drawn into the still, focused place of prayer, the reflections bring a sense of harmony and peace. God's Shalom.

The booklet reminds me of one of the places where I used to pray on this particular retreat. In the cottage where I stayed, one of the rooms had been converted into a 'chapel'. I would kneel or lie prostrate on the floor of that chapel and gaze at the map of the world that covered the wall opposite me. A picture of Mary adoring the Christ-child nestled in the corner of the map while, over Cyprus, where I live, hung an illuminated circle on which was inscribed God's promise: 'I shall put my Spirit in you.' A picture and a promise that reminded me of some of the ways God had persuaded me to embrace the world.

'Do share some of your own prayers,' James Catford insisted when I agreed to work on this project. At first, I balked at this request. For me, prayer is intensely personal. Much of it is conducted in silence. Most of it is wordless. So I feared there would be little to quote. When I do write prayers, I write them for God, not for publication. Most are therefore not publishable. The prayers that appear in this book, therefore, are not polished poetry or prose, but words that my pen has whispered to God. Some were written on the retreats I have mentioned. Others, during equally life-changing moments of my prayer pilgrimage. I share them for one reason only – because there are times in my life when I am stuck for words to pray or when the stream of my own spontaneous, wordless prayer dries up or when I simply sense the rightness of approaching God through words penned by others under the inspiration of the Holy Spirit. Time and time again, I have found that those who have penned their prayers, whether they lived thousands of years ago or whether they are my contemporaries, have breathed the prayer my heart yearns to pray. With relief, I echo them, personalising them in such a way that I can make of them an offering to God. I quote some of these prayers in this book alongside my own. If any of my prayers are ever treasured by my readers in the way I treasure some of the prayers I have quoted, I shall be both humbled and joyful.

Joyce Huggett

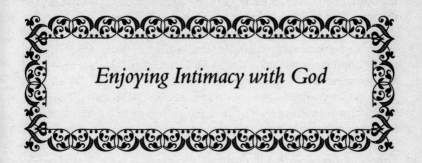

Enjoying Intimacy with God

The desire to sacrifice for Christ, for some people, is born in the place of intimacy with God. I sense we see this happening in the life of Mary of Bethany (see Luke 10:38–41). When her gregarious sister, Martha, invited Jesus into their home, Mary found herself drawn by Jesus's magnetism to nestle at his feet. There, doubtless, she found herself on the receiving end of his love for, wherever Jesus went, love flowed from him. John makes it clear in his Gospel that Mary reciprocated the Master's love. One way she expressed her adoration was to anoint Jesus with her most precious possession: the perfume she was probably saving for her wedding day.

Did Jesus share with her, in those moments of delicious intimacy, the reason why he was visiting Bethany at that moment in time? Did he tell her what he had been attempting for months to impress on his disciples: that he was on his way to Jerusalem where he would be butchered to death? It seems probable that he did divulge these secrets. Is that not the reason why, in John 12, we find Mary sidling alongside Jesus at the supper party? Is that not the reason why she prepared him for his burial with that memorable sacrifice that filled the air with its fragrance?

According to Jesus, Mary had discovered 'the one essential thing' (Luke 10:42) – the value of soaking up, absorbing, personalising the elixir of the divine Love. It was as she drank these draughts of love and later feasted on them by pondering them that her heart was stirred and she conceived the desire to express her devotion in self-sacrificing service – even taking the risk of doing so in public.

As for Mary, so for us. When we create time to assimilate the fact that we are God's cherished children, little by little, our hearts lose their hardness. In the soft centre of our being the desire to sacrifice self for the Beloved is born. One reason for this is that, where true love exists, it yearns to please and promote the well-being of the loved one. Another reason is that, when we both grasp and digest the love of another, we hear that healing, liberating message: we are accepted, valued, wanted. This message nourishes, nurtures and affirms us in such a way that it generates within us the desire to achieve great things for the loved one – albeit in a hidden, humble way. That is why the first section of this book consists of murmurings written by those who have lingered in the presence of God, relished intimacy with him and yearned for an even deeper relationship with him. Such intimacy can, of course, be sought as an escape from the harsh realities of life, but if the intimacy being enjoyed is truly with Christ, the Saviour of the world, his compassion for a weary world will, in time, rub off on us. His compassion is contagious. The closer we come to him, the closer we shall identify with his heart's longing to rescue the world and those that live in it.

Some of the prayers are simple, ordinary, even domestic. Others are more majestic, even grand. Each of them begs the would-be pray-er to read them as slowly as possible – to savour them, where appropriate to echo them or to allow them to trigger a prayer of their own.

LIKE MARY

A woman in the crowd called out, 'Blessed is the mother who gave you birth and nursed you.' Jesus replied: 'Blessed rather are those who hear the word of God and obey it.' — *Luke 11:27, 28*

I am the Lord, your Saviour ...
I want you to enter into my love.
Yes, I want you to come so close to me that
I can speak my love into your heart.

I want to come to you as I came to Mary.
I look on you as I looked on Mary.

I am not looking at your greatness
nor at your attempts at asserting yourself
or trying to stand out from others.
I see your littleness.
I see deep within you —
behind all your various disguises,
masks and roles —
I see the child,
My beloved child who is hungry and cries
for My love.
Come to Me.
Rest in Me.
Stay with Me ...

I am the Lord, your Saviour.
I want to come to you now and enfold you with my love
on all sides.

I do not want to drill My love into your life.
I want to bring it to birth in you.

Mary's task is yours too.
To receive Jesus into your life and to bring
My love to birth into your world.
In that way I can use you as a channel
for My love.

Through you I can love the people I send
in your path.
I can use *your eyes* to look at them
with my goodness.
I can use *your ears* to listen to them.
I can use *your mouth* to speak to them.

Rest now *in My Love*.
Then I can do great things for you too.
And through you.

      – *Sr Lisbeth CHN, transl.* [1]

LOVE

Lord my God, when Your love spilled over
    into creation
        You thought of me.
          I am
from love,   of love,   for love.
    Let my heart, O God, always
        recognise,
           cherish,
          and enjoy your goodness in all of creation.
    Direct all that is me toward your praise.
Teach me reverence for every person, all things,
    energise me in your service.
               Lord God,
may nothing ever distract me from your love ...
    neither health nor sickness,
        wealth nor poverty,
        honour nor dishonour,
        long life nor short life.
May I never seek nor choose to be other
    than You intend or wish.

– *Jacqueline Syrup Bergan and
S. Marie Schwan* [2]

Mary sat at the feet of Jesus and listened. She soaked up Jesus's love and responded with reciprocal love. Love prompted her to act – to donate to Jesus her most precious possession. We, too, may sit at the feet of Christ and absorb his love. Unlike Mary, we cannot anoint the feet of the Beloved. We can, however, touch and minister to the needs of the poor instead knowing that, whatever we do for the least of Christ's brothers or sisters, we do for him.

> You yourself are my contemplation;
> You are my delight.
> You for your own sake
> I seek above me;
> from you yourself I feed within me.
> You are the field in which I labour;
> You are the fruit for which I labour.
> You are my cause;
> You are my effect.
> You are my beginning;
> You are my end without end.
> You are for me eternity

> – *My adaptation of a prayer of*
> *Isaac of Stella, 1100–69*

ALL IN ALL

True knowledge of Me comes when I am *valued* ... To place Me above everything else in your life is indispensable to your growth ... causing you to *thrill* at the thought of Me, and to desire closer and closer communion with Me.

When you arrive at the blessed state of My being all in all to you, you also realise that this has not made any *less* precious those whom you love on earth ... On the contrary, My place of supremacy in your life encircles those other ties, and means that the influence of heaven is in your relationships – making them pleasing to Me.

> – *John Woolley* [3]

O Lord our God,
Whose might is invincible,
Whose glory is incomprehensible,
Whose mercy is immeasurable
and Whose love towards mankind is unspeakable ...
look down upon us ...
and show us Your abundant mercy and compassion.

*— My adaptation of the First Prayer from
the Liturgy of St John Chrysostom*

O Gracious and holy Father
give us wisdom to perceive you,
intelligence to understand you,
diligence to seek you,
eyes to behold you,
a life to proclaim you,
and a heart to meditate on you,
through the power of the Spirit of Jesus Christ our Lord.

— St Benedict

Lord Jesus our Saviour,
    let us now come to you;
our hearts are cold;
    Lord, warm them by your selfless love;
our hearts are sinful;
    cleanse them with your precious blood.
Our hearts are weak;
    strengthen them with your joyous Spirit.
Our hearts are empty;
    fill them with your divine presence.

Lord Jesus, our hearts are yours;
    possess them always
    and only for
    yourself.

— St Augustine of Hippo

You shone upon me with brilliant radiance and, so it seemed, you appeared to me in your wholeness as with my whole self I gazed openly upon you. And when I said, 'Master, who are you?' then you were pleased to speak for the first time with me the prodigal. With what gentleness did you talk to me, as I stood astonished and trembling, as I reflected a little within myself and said: 'What does this glory and this dazzling brightness mean? How is it that I am chosen to receive such great blessings?'

'I am God,' you replied, 'who became man for your sake; and because you have sought me with your whole heart, see from this time onwards you shall be my brother, my fellow-heir, and my friend.'

> − *St Symeon the New Theologian,*
> *eleventh century*

Come, my Light, and illumine my darkness.
Come, my Life, and revive me from death.
Come, my Physician, and heal my wounds.
Come, Flame of divine love,
and burn up the thorns of my sins, kindling my heart with the
flame of thy love.
Come, my King, sit upon the throne of my heart and reign there.
For thou alone art my King and my Lord.

> − *St Dimitri of Rostov,*
> *Russian seventeenth-century Bishop*

I know that the Immovable comes down;
I know that the Invisible appears to me;
I know that he who is far outside the whole creation
takes me within himself and hides me in his arms …
I, a frail, small mortal in the world,
behold the Creator of the world, all of him, within myself;
and I know that I shall not die, for I am within the Life,
I have the whole of Life springing up as a fountain within me.
You are within my heart, you are in heaven:
both there and here you show yourself to me with equal glory.

> − *My adaptation of a prayer of St*
> *Symeon the New Theologian*

MOTHER GOD

> I have stilled and quietened my soul;
> like a weaned child with its mother,
> like a weaned child is my soul
> within me.
>
> — *Psalm 131:2*

Lord,
hold me as a mother holds her baby
because you love me.
Not because I'm hurt or sick,
but just because you love me.
Caress my forehead.
Gaze tenderly into my eyes.
Kiss me.
Rock me gently and sing me a love song.
Teach me, Lord, to love you as a child loves its mother;
To rest in you as a baby rests in its mother's arms,
                     its mother's lap —
content and completely fulfilled.

— *SCW*

RELAX IN MY LOVE

If you are consciously relaxing in my love, others can truly receive
me through yourself. You are then a source of joy, reassurance and
peace to them.

— *John Woolley* [4]

HOLD ME CLOSE

Often, we're not able to reach out to others because we are hurting too much ourselves. When we know that God cherishes us in the way this prayer describes, the nature of our service may well change. We no longer serve out of duty or for the fun of fulfilment. We serve from desire.

Hold me close, Lord;
I so easily feel alone-ness.
May I be aware of your ever-present reality in my life.

My child —
I chose you;
I planned for you;
I brought you into being.
I gave you to your family;
I entrusted you to them,
though my heart ached
to know that I could not protect you
from all the knocks and hurts that would come.

I've walked beside you all the way;
I've walked behind and gone before,
and walked by your side.
Nothing has come to you that I didn't know about.
Though the enemy would have mauled you
as a lion mauls a lamb
or a bear cub,
I never let him.

Trust me, trust me,
know that I love you,
know that I care deeply for one who is mine,
mine,
MINE.

           – SCW

GOD OUR MOTHER

And you, Jesus, are you not also a mother?
      Are you not the mother, who, like a hen,
      gathers her chickens under her wings...

And you, my soul, dead in yourself,
      run under the wings of Jesus your mother
      and lament your griefs under his feathers.
      Ask that your wounds may be healed
      and that, comforted, you may live again.

Christ, my mother,
      you gather your chickens under your wings;
this dead chicken of yours puts himself under those wings.
For by your gentleness the badly frightened are comforted,
      by your sweet smell the despairing are revived,
      your warmth gives life to the dead,
      your touch justifies sinners.
      Mother, know again your dead [child],
both by the sign of the cross and the voice of confession.
      Warm your chicken...
          justify your sinner.
      Let your terrified one be consoled by you;
      despairing of himself, let [her] be comforted by you;
      and in your whole and unceasing grace
      let [her] be refashioned by you.
      For from you flows consolation for sinners;
      to you be blessing for ages and ages. Amen.

*   — St Anselm, 1070, abbreviated version*

AVAILABLE FOR YOU

Lord,
I offer what I am
to what You are.
I stretch up to You in desire
my attention on You alone.
I cannot grasp You
     explain You
     describe You
Only cast myself into the depths
     of your mystery
Only let your love pierce the
     cloud of my unknowing.
Let me forget all but You
You are what I long for
You are my chiefest good
You are my eager hope
You are my allness.

In the glimpses of your Eternity
     Your Unconditional Freedom
     Your Unfailing Wisdom
     Your Perfect Love
I am humble and worshipping
     warming to love and hope
     waiting and available
     for your Will
     dear Lord.

           — *George Appleton* [5]

YOUR SERVANT IS LISTENING

Speak, Lord, for your servant is listening.
O, Lord, my heart is ready,
my mind awake, attentive, alert;
my spirit open and ardent,
abandoning all else,
holding itself in leash,
straining the eye of faith,
hearkening for your step, distant and nearer,
leaping with love,
throbbing loudly, yet lying still.

Speak, Lord, for your servant is listening.

> — *My adaptation of a prayer of*
> *Dean Eric Milner-White* [6]

MY LIFE, MY ALL

O Jesus,
you are my life,
my beloved,
my all.
I offer my life,
I give you my heart,
I wish what you wish,
nothing but your holy will.

> — *Mary Euphrasia* [7]

FOLLOWING JESUS

Dear Lord and Father of mankind,
forgive our foolish ways.
Re-clothe us in our rightful mind,
in purer lives thy service find,
in deeper reverence, praise.

In simple trust like theirs who heard,
beside the Syrian sea,
the gracious calling of the Lord,
let us, like them, without a word,
rise up and follow thee.

Drop thy still dews of quietness,
Till all our strivings cease:
Take from our souls the strain and stress,
And let our ordered lives confess
The beauty of thy peace.

> *— John Greenleaf Whittier,*
> *1807–92*

SPIRIT-FILLED BUT HUNGRY

Jesu, Thou joy of loving hearts,
Thou fount of life, Thou light of men,
From the best bliss that earth imparts,
We turn unfilled to Thee again.

> *— Twelfth century*

AT PEACE

You are my peace, O Lord.
From the thousand wearinesses of the day-to-day,
from the disappointments,
from the nervous and senseless haste,
I turn to you
and am at peace.
The clamour dies.
I spring to life in the sunshine of your presence.
Even so, come, Lord Jesus
to this heart of mine.

– LJH

THIRSTING FOR GOD'S PRESENCE

Dear Lord,
teach me to pray.
For just as the deer pants for cool water
so my heart hungers for you.
My soul is parched and dry;
I thirst for Your presence, my Living Lord.
I will carve out a place for you.
Lord, hear my prayer.
In that place,
in every place,
come to me and meet me.

– LJH

THE FOCUS OF GOD'S LOVE

Father,
In this place of prayer
I feel your everlasting arms
enfolding me
caressing me
cradling me
in the embrace of never-ending love.
For your tenderness
I praise you
that I am the focus of your love.
I thank you
and surrender myself to you,
though all too feeble
is my response of love to Love.

– LJH

SUSTENANCE AND SUSTAINER

Beloved –
I need you.
Without you I cannot exist.
You are my sustenance
and my Sustainer.
Turn me from all lesser loves
to Love.
Succour and strengthen me
tonight and always.
Amen.

– LJH

YOU CAME

All day long on my bed
I looked for the one my heart loves;
I looked for him but did not find him.
I will get up now and ... search for the one my heart loves.
So I looked for him but did not find him.
The watchmen found me
as they made their rounds in the city.
'Have you seen the one my heart loves?'
Scarcely had I passed them
when I found the one my heart loves.
I held him and would not let him go
till I had brought him to my mother's house
to the room of the one who conceived me.

> — *My adaptation of the Song of*
> *Songs 3:1–4*

I had just written that when he came:

> Silently, surreptitiously,
> he overwhelmed me
> ravished me
> held me.
> He loved me,
> filled me,
> and he left me.
> But I am no longer bereft,
> just dazed.
> Enraptured.
> Re-captivated.
> Conquered.
> Lost in wonder,
>   love
>   and praise.

No words,
    no music,
        no drawing
can express this inexpressible joy.
Only wonder.
    Only love.
        Only praise.
            Only the sounds of silent adoration.

ENJOYING INTIMACY AT ALL TIMES

Lord of my heart, give me vision to inspire me,
that working or resting, I may always think of you;
Lord of my heart, give me light to guide me,
that at home or abroad, I may always walk in your way;
Lord of my heart, give me wisdom to direct me,
that thinking or acting, I may always discern right from wrong;
Lord of my heart, give me courage to strengthen me,
that amongst friends or enemies, I may always proclaim your justice;
Lord of my heart, give me trust to console me,
that hungry or well-fed, I may always rely on your mercy;
Heart of my own heart, whatever may befall me,
rule over my thoughts and feelings, my words and actions. Amen.

                    –   *Source unknown*

REMEMBERING

The following was written at a time when I was recalling God's goodness to us in the aftermath of a car crash in the former Yugoslavia. Our Dormobile was a write-off so we were forced to travel home by train. When journeying through Italy, an unknown passenger came up to my husband and pressed into his hand some £20 worth of lire so that we could buy food for the journey. Earlier in the trip, Yugoslav peasants had shared their picnic with us.

For every memory of your faithfulness
my Father,
I give you thanks and praise.
When we were destitute,
you proved yourself to be an abundant God.
Aware, afresh,
of the length and breadth,
the height and depth
of your love,
I pray that, even now,
my roots may be burrowing ever deeper
into the love that will not let me go
so that, when changes shake those roots,
my trust in you may remain strong and firm.

— *LJH*

SOLITUDE

Solitude at last.
Beauty.
Tranquillity.
Familiarity.
Shalom.
Soft songs sung by birds.

In this place where your peace permeates my pain,
and where I feel the gravitational pull of Love, Lord,
I begin to feel,
not fragmented,
but focused,
in harmony with you,
with your creation,
with my situation.
I begin to gain a new perspective –
your perspective.
I begin to enter into your REST.
For this, I give you heart-felt thanks
and praise.

         – *LJH*

TEACH ME TO LISTEN

Teach me to listen, Lord
for your voice –
in busyness and in boredom,
in certainty and in doubt,
in noise and in silence.

         – *John Veltri SJ* [8]

THE PEARL OF GREAT PRICE

You, O Lord, are the One that I long for.
And yet
I'm not sure that I can bear the emptiness
that this longing will involve.
If I really long for you
then there will be no room
for the clutter of a lot of other longings.

I must be hollowed out
to become a capacity for you.
I shrink from the pain that that will involve.
But I must needs feel the poverty of my emptiness
and my poverty meets with your giving
in the silence of lovers.

I feel this emptiness as an ache,
a frustration
as I realise that what I want, dear Lord,
more than anything else in the world
is that my life should revolve around YOU,
the pearl of great price;
that I should be able to take others deeper into you;
that I might be able to take your love into the hearts of others.
Give me the grace to go on and on
wanting you more than anything or anyone.

> — *LJH: I have added the last verse to the*
> *previous two from an unknown source*

GOD'S LOVE (1)

Father,
I pray that out of the wealth of your glory
You will strengthen my inner being with your Spirit,
so that Christ will make his home in my heart
and so that I may have my roots in love
and make love the foundation
of my entire existence.
I pray that You will reveal to me
just how broad and long,
how high and deep
the love of Christ is,
so that I may be filled to overflowing
with the very nature of Christ.

–   My adaptation of Ephesians 3:14–21

GOD'S LOVE (2)

Lord, your love is a persevering love
that brings me back,
that renews a sense of perspective,
that woos and wins me again and again.
For this undeserved, unearned gift,
I feel eternally grateful.

–   LJH

A PRAYER OF ST AUGUSTINE

Late have I loved you, O beauty ever ancient, ever new!
Late have I loved you
and behold, you were within, and I without,
        and without I sought you.
And deformed, I ran after those forms of beauty
        you have made.
You were with me, and I was not with you,
those things held me back from you,
things whose only being was to be in you.
You called;
you cried;
and broke in through my deafness.
You flashed;
you shone;
and you chased away my blindness.
You became fragrant;
and I inhaled and sighed for you.
I tasted,
and now hunger and thirst for you.
You touched me;
and I burned for your embrace.

DAY BY DAY

O gentle flame of the life of Christ,
enfold and fill my heart afresh
as each new day is born.

— *Sister Theresa Margaret CHN*

PSALM 139

O God, you know me inside out
    through and through.

Everything I do
    every thought that flits through my mind
    every step I take
    every plan I make
    every word I speak
you know, even before these things happen.

You know my past.
You know my future.

Your circumventing presence covers my every move.
Your knowledge of me sometimes comforts me,
    sometimes frightens me,
    but always it is far beyond my comprehension.

There is no way to escape you, no place to hide.
If I ascend to the heights of joy
    you are there before me.
If I am plunged into the depths of despair
    you are there to meet me.
I could fly to the other side of the world
    and find you there to lead the way.
I could walk into the darkest of nights
    only to find you there
    to lighten its dismal hours.

You were present at my very conception.
You guided the moulding of my unformed members
    within the body of my mother.
Nothing about me, from beginning to end
    was hid from your eyes.
How wonderful it all is.

May your all-knowing, everywhere-present Spirit
continue to search out my feelings and thoughts.
Deliver me from all that may hurt or destroy me
and guide me along the paths of love and truth.

– *Source unknown*

Help Me to Say Yes

We are intimately loved long before our parents, teachers, spouses, children and friends loved or wounded us. That's the truth of our lives. That's the truth I want you to claim for yourself. That's the truth spoken by the voice that says, 'You are my Beloved.'

Listening to that voice with great inner attentiveness, I hear at my centre words that say: 'I have called you by name, from the very beginning. You are mine and I am yours. You are my Beloved, on you my favour rests. I have moulded you in the depths of the earth and knitted you together in your mother's womb. I have carved you in the palms of my hands and hidden you in the shadow of my embrace. I look at you with infinite tenderness and care for you with a care more intimate than that of a mother for her child. I have counted every hair on your head and guided you at every step. Wherever you go, I go with you, and wherever you rest, I keep watch. I will give you food that will satisfy all your hunger and drink that will quench all your thirst. I will not hide my face from you. You know me as your own as I know you as my own. You belong to me … Wherever you are I will be. Nothing will ever separate us. We are one.'

Every time you listen with great attentiveness to that voice that calls you the Beloved, you will discover within yourself a desire to hear that voice longer and more deeply. It is like discovering a well in the desert. Once you have touched wet ground, you want to dig deeper.

— Henri Nouwen [1]

When we know ourselves loved like that by God, slowly but surely, by the grace of God's Spirit, our hearts are stirred. We love in return. That is what we observed at the beginning of the first section of this book.

Unlike Mary of Bethany, however, when our hearts have been warmed by the divine Love, we cannot anoint the head or wash the feet of God himself. What we can do, instead, is to listen in the hushed and hidden places of our heart. Listen to his Word, listen to his longings, listen to his heartbeat. As we listen, Jesus's great parable of the sheep and the goats may well be brought into our awareness:

When the Son of Man comes in his glory, and all the angels with him, he will sit on his throne in heavenly glory. All the nations will be gathered before him, and he will separate the people one from another as a shepherd separates the sheep from the goats. He will put the sheep on his right and the goats on his left.

Then the King will say to those on his right, 'Come, you who are blessed by my Father; take your inheritance, the kingdom prepared for you since the creation of the world. For I was hungry and you gave me something to eat, I was thirsty and you gave me something to drink, I was a stranger and you invited me in, I needed clothes and you clothed me, I was sick and you looked after me, I was in prison and you came to visit me.'

Then the righteous will answer him, 'Lord, when did we see you hungry and feed you, or thirsty and give you something to drink? When did we see you a stranger and invite you in, or needing clothes and clothe you? When did we see you sick or in prison and go to visit you?' The King will reply, 'I tell you the truth, whatever you did for one of the least of these brothers of mine, you did for me.'

– Matt. 25:31–40

As we ponder this passage, the message becomes inescapably clear. Jean Vanier sums it up memorably when he reminds us that the clear call of Christ, to some of us, is to leave everything – and to become beggars of compassion like St Francis of Assisi. He invites others to leave their familiar surroundings so that they can more effectively share their lives with the poor and weak. Still others, he calls to invite into their hearts and homes, an elderly neighbour, a handicapped child or others similarly impoverished.

As we see through stories like the Good Samaritan, Jesus calls each of us to incarnate his compassion wherever we find ourselves. Startlingly and memorably, Jean Vanier claims:

> The poor and the weak have revealed to me
> the great secret of Jesus.
> If you wish to follow him
> you must not try to climb the ladder of success and power,
> becoming more and more important.
> Instead, you must walk *down* the ladder,
> to meet and walk with people
> who are broken and in pain.
> The light is there, shining in the darkness,

in the darkness of their poverty.
The poor with whom you are called to share your life
are perhaps the sick and the old;
people out of work,
young people caught up in the world of drugs,
people angry because they were terribly hurt
when they were young,
people with disabilities or sick with AIDS,
or just out of prison;
people in slums or ghettos,
people in far-off lands
where there is much hunger and suffering,
people who are oppressed
because of the colour of their skin,
people who are lonely in overcrowded cities,
people in pain.

— *Jean Vanier* [2]

When the call came to me to leave the cottage that I love, my country and my culture, my reaction was mixed. I was in touch with awe. I was also in touch with excitement. But the predominant feeling was of fear: would I be able to cope? My 'Yes' was whispered only after a struggle. Others have been prepared to utter a more resounding 'Yes' than mine. The prayers in this section begin with God's plaintive, persistent call. They continue by reflecting the joy and the pain, the anticipation and the fear with which Christians down the ages have expressed their willingness and readiness to serve God by serving his people — whether at home or in distant lands.

SAYING YES

This was written after meditating on the Annunciation, sitting with the Holy Trinity in the heavenly places and contemplating a world hurtling to destruction.

Mary,
like clay in the potter's hands,
soft, malleable, yielding,
you inspire me to say yes.

Holy Trinity,
like birds brooding over their young
watching, waiting, wondering,
bring to birth my yes.

Father
like a lover longing for the loved one,
wooing, giving, sacrificing,
strengthen my yes.

Jesus,
Father's delight, Father's darling,
a foetus in a woman's womb
give me the grace to say yes.

Holy Spirit,
co-Creator of the universe,
energy flowing from the Father,
empower me to say yes.

Mary
still the same
yet strangely different
nurturing the Saviour-seed
carrying your secret wherever you go
teach me to say yes
       not one yes
             but a thousand yeses
                a new yes

with every new morning
and every turn of the road
that I, too, may become part of this MYSTERY:
our Master's plan
for the salvation of the world.

– LJH

MY NEW MISSION

Going, not in the spring-time of my years
but in the late summer.
Ripened, with a wrinkle here and there
and the odd grey hair!
Going, not with the daring of youth
but with the calm of mid life . . .
In touch with the weaknesses,
aware of the strengths.
Going, not with the idealism of the young
but bringing the realism of experience …
Shaped by life's dyings
by her life-giving loves.
I need your compassion, Lord, to go with
a listening, trusting, feeling heart,
receptive, patient, a love filled with passion …
compassion for your people.
Going, knowing I come only with God and me.
Coming, to discover their God and them.

– Barbara Cameron [4]

LOVING HEART

Will you be the one who will serve Me intensely?
Will you listen to the heart cries of your neighbour
    after everyone else has walked away ... ?
Will you be the one who stays up longest to hear his woeful
    story?
Will you be the one to look longest
    for some trace of Me in the desolate,
    the derelict,
    the alcoholic?
Will you try to find some resemblance of the Father
    in the one who slanders you?
Will you be the one to keep on loving even when the love is
    unrequited?
Will you ask others in to share your meal
    when there is no assurance of your next meal?
Will you go forth and console others
    when your own need of consolation is beyond tears?
Will you forgive others
    even though others refuse to forgive you?
Care, when no one cares;
    love, when no one loves;
    fill others from your own emptiness?
Could you rather pardon than be pardoned;
    could you rather like than be liked;
    love, rather than be loved?
Understand, rather than be understood?
Can you accept insult,
    and give forth praise in exchange ...
    take ridicule and give forth understanding in exchange?
Will you listen attentively
    even though your own problems are thundering
    in your heart?
Will you speak lovingly of My will
    even when it has crushed you?
Then, surrendered heart,
minister to My people in pure love.

* − Joan Hutson* [3]

DEDICATION

This was written as a result of meditating on a number of Bible passages in succession: Matt. 25:31–46; Jesus's clear statement: 'The Son of Man is going to be betrayed and crucified' (Matt. 26:2) and the anointing at Bethany (Matt. 26:6–13)

Suffering One,
>> I hold to you all that I have
>> and all that I am
> that your love would flow, not just into me
>> but through me
> to caress and bless
>> the lives of others.
> For, Beloved Bridegroom
>> I love you
>> and would minister to you
>> if I could.
>> I do it in the only way I know
>> by ministering to others
>> in your name.

Loved one,
>> I receive your offering of love
>> your dedication of self;
> you will watch, with awe, while I break you
>> and use you
> by distributing you in far-flung places.
> You have only to trust
>> and rest
> and you will be blessed
> and become an ever-increasing blessing,
> reaping a rich harvest
>> for my Kingdom.

– *LJH*

Lord,
I know not what I ought to ask of you.
You only know what I need.
You know me better than I know myself . . .
Teach me to pray.
Pray yourself in me.

– *Archbishop François Fénelon*

JESUS

This was written as a result of meditating on the Temptations of Jesus in the wilderness and becoming acutely aware of his youthfulness, yet his sense of purpose and direction.

Jesus,
young,
strong,
sensitive,
powerful,
God–man.
Teach me to live as you lived:
with only one desire –
to be God's person
    at God's moment
        in the right place at the right time
      poised
          like an athlete waiting for
          the starting gun
ready to flex every nerve and muscle
      until the race is won.

– *LJH*

A PRAYER OF ABANDONMENT

Father, I abandon myself into your hands;
      do with me what you will.
Whatever you may do, I accept all.
Let only your will be done in me,
      and in all your creatures –
      I wish no more than this, O Lord.
Into your hands I commend my soul;
      I offer it to you with all the love of my heart,
      for I love you, Lord, and so need to give myself,
      to surrender myself into your hands without reserve,
      and with boundless confidence,
      for you are my Father.

– Charles de Foucauld

LIKE JESUS

Lord Jesus, teach me to be generous,
to serve you as you deserve to be served;
to give and not to count the cost;
to fight and not to heed the wounds;
to toil and not to seek for rest;
to labour and to ask for no reward,
save that of knowing that I do your holy will.

– St Ignatius of Loyola

LOST AND FOUND

Written as a result of meditating on the parables about 'lost things': lost coin, lost sheep, lost sons from Luke 15:

Beloved,

for searching for me
as the Middle Eastern woman
    searched for her silver coin
I adore you.
For leaving the splendours of heaven
to lift me from the thicket
I honour you.
For turning me
    from an alien
                into a member of God's family
I give you heartfelt praise.

Father,

for sparing your Son
I worship you.
For giving me the grace to see
I give you praise.
For impressing your truths on me
    as thumbs make their imprint on soft clay
I give you humble and heartfelt thanks
    and offer you
            all that I am
                all that I have
                    all that I can become
for you to use
as you choose
from now
    and into eternity.

– *LJH*

TURN ME, LORD

One of the prayers that I pray most regularly is a short one popularised by St Ignatius of Loyola. One variation of it is: 'Turn my whole being to your praise and service.' While praying these words one day, I added a longer prayer of my own.

Whatever it costs, Beloved,
turn my whole being to your praise and service,
keep me from becoming blind or deaf,
    stupid or cunning.
        Limited.
Rather, cause me to abandon all to you.
For, at the deepest level of my being,
heart-hunger gives rise to a heart-cry:
'Don't ask me to leave you
nor to refrain from following after you.
Where you go,
I will go ...'

Here and now,
I offer to you
all that I have
and all that I am.
If it means accepting abuse or poverty
so be it.
I commit myself to you
'for better, for worse,
for richer for poorer,
in sickness and in health'
accepting all, whatever you choose to send,
using all,
welcoming all,
knowing that it comes gift-wrapped
with love from you.

Echoing those truths penned by Ramon Lull:
'What is the greatest darkness?
The absence of my Beloved.
And what is the greatest light?
The presence of my Beloved.'

– LJH

CALLED

I know
that I am called.
The message was quite clear
and yet I cannot see
the how, the why.

I feel so small, so weak,
so ill equipped
for such a task.
And yet I am prepared
to say my yes
and undertake the risk
and enter the unknown
responding to the call.
Trustfully treading my way
the only one
that leads to life –
to Him.

– HenryRohr [5]

ALL IS OF YOU

Jesus, may all that is you flow into me,
may your body and blood be my food and drink.
May your passion and death be my strength and life.
Jesus, with you by my side enough has been given.
May the shelter I seek be the shadow of your cross.
Let me not run from the love which you offer,
but hold me safe from the forces of evil.
On each of my dyings shed your light and love.
Keep calling me until that day comes
when, with your saints, I may praise you for ever.

And Jesus, while I walk this earth
remind me often
that my resources do not come from me
they simply flow through me.
You are the Giver
I am simply the receptacle,
        the supplier.
This awareness excites,
        strengthens
                and encourages me.
The realisation that I am never the source
of an insight,
        a book,
                or an inspiration
humbles me.
It challenges me to abide
                to wait
                to listen,
for all
        all
        ALL –
        is of you.

                    – LJH
                    except verse 1: 'The Soul of Christ' [6]

THE BODY OF CHRIST

Whenever I pray this prayer, my mind goes to the church where members of the St Egidio Community in Rome meet to pray. There, hanging on the wall, is a crucifix that seemed to draw me to itself. The body of Christ has no arms and no legs. When I asked a member of the community why it hung there, he said: 'We hang it here to remind us that, today, Christ has no hands but our hands and no feet but our feet.'

Lord Jesus, I give you my hands to do your work.
I give you my feet to go your way.
I give you my eyes to see as you do.
I give you my tongue to speak your words.
I give you my mind that you may think in me.
I give you my spirit that you may pray in me.
Above all, I give you my heart
that you may love in me your Father and all mankind.
I give you my whole self that you may grow in me so that
        it is you, Lord Jesus,
who live and work and pray in me.

— *A Grail prayer printed on a prayer card*

FOR YOU ALONE

Dear Lord and Saviour, Jesus Christ,
I hold up all my weakness to your strength,
my failure to your faithfulness,
my sinfulness to your perfection,
my loneliness to your compassion,
my little pains to your great agony on the Cross.

I pray that you will cleanse me,
      strengthen me,
            GUIDE ME,
so that in all ways my life may be lived
as you would have it lived,
without cowardice,
and for you alone.
Show me how to live in true humility,
      true contrition
           and true love.

>   — *Found on a prayer card*
>   *with the initials M.S.*

THE REFUGEE

At harvest time in the part of Cyprus where I live, field mice and rats are hounded from their homes by harvesters. Since we live in the corner of a field, they seem to take a liking to our home and garden at this time of year. The task of controlling them is onerous and sometimes distressing. The rat I describe seemed menacing until I watched it die!

Diligent harvesters demolished its home;
it came seeking a niche in mine,
but its behaviour proved unacceptable.
It cut the cable of my modem with its scissor-sharp teeth.
It pierced the hose linking the washing machine to the water supply
and flooded the floor.
I set up a witch-hunt for it,
fed it with dishes full of pretty poison.
I determined to drive it from my home
by killing it.

Tonight it lay listless on the patio,
its little paws were bleeding.
It washed its face for the last time –
in blood.
Then it crept into a corner to hide – to die.
The bloody paw marks on the patio stared up at me,
persuading me that the little creature, now so harmless, must be
                    hurting.
I heard the Beloved's voice reminding me
that the Father cares about each falling sparrow,
and my heart was suddenly sorrowful.
I had deliberately killed one of God's creatures.

Maybe rats have to be exterminated, Lord,
but what about those other refugees,
the ones I watched on television today
running helplessly from their homes
clutching only one bundle of belongings
By my negligence
and dismissal of their plight,

by keeping them out of my heart and home
because their behaviour might not be acceptable
am I, by any chance, killing them too?

May I feel the pain of the displaced.
May it prompt me to be to them
what you would have me be,
Dear Light of the World.

– LJH

DESERT FERTILITY

Spirit of Life,
    hover over me, breathe life into me, empower me,
bring to birth the seeds of love, and peace, and compassion
    growing in me.
Make me fertile with the seeds of the fruits of the Spirit:
    nourish them, nurture them, ripen them into fruitfulness.
Pour out your Spirit on the gifts, your gifts, you have
    given me that I may prophesy and dream dreams and see
    visions as you promised.
Breathe life into me in abundance
    and let it flow from me abundantly.
Spirit of Life,
    flow through me powerfully, vitally
    that my presence to others may always be life-giving.
    Continue to be born in me, to bring me to birth
    every day, increasing my capacity for love,
    for peace, for compassion, for abundance,
    for gratitude, for living life
    and bringing life to others.

– Barbara Cameron [7]

THE FRAGRANCE OF CHRIST

Dear Jesus,
help me to spread your fragrance
everywhere I go.
Flood my soul with your spirit and life.
Penetrate and possess my whole being so utterly
that my life may only be a radiance of yours.
Shine through me,
and so be in me,
that every soul I come in contact with
may feel your presence.
Let them look up and see
no longer me but only Jesus.
Stay with me,
and then I shall begin to shine
as you shine
so to shine as to be a light to others;
the light, O Jesus,
will be all from you,
none of it will be mine;
it will be you shining on others through me.
Let me praise you in the way you love best
by shining on those around me.
Let me preach you,
not by words only,
but by the catching force of example,
the evident fullness
of the love my heart bears to you.

— *Mother Teresa of Calcutta:*
   adapted from Cardinal Newman [8]

JESUS, MY LEADER

Jesus,
I see you as you were as a youth
and a young leader:
strong, vigorous, full of integrity,
with the best interests of people at heart,
with the burning desire to make life better
for everyone
so that all could come into your Kingdom.
I want to follow you, Lord.
I want to take you as my leader.
I want to improve the lot
of those who are being exploited.
Lead me.
Guide our steps
to that place where we can be most effective
for you in reaching out to others.

Holy Spirit,
Thank you for opening my eyes to see Jesus
        as he really is:
a person with a cutting edge.
Change me into his likeness
that I may be a sharp tool in his hands
whatever it costs.
Continue to open my eyes until I see him
as he really is.

– *LJH*

YOURS

Majestic Sovereign, timeless wisdom,
your kindness melts my hard, cold soul.
Handsome lover, selfless giver,
your beauty fills my dull, sad eyes.
I am yours, you made me,
I am yours, you called me,
I am yours, you saved me,
I am yours, you loved me,
I will never leave your presence.
Give me death, give me life,
give me sickness, give me health,
give me honour, give me shame,
give me weakness, give me strength,
I will have whatever you give.

– St Teresa of Avila

OPEN TO GOD

Prise open my fingers
        O God
that nothing:
        my cottage
                my country
                        my culture
and no one:
        my children
                my companions
                        my confidantes
may keep me
        from being radically open
                to you
or prevent me from
        saying yes to you.

– LJH

There will be times when you will not see the immediate way ahead. You may be filled with panic, wanting to avoid what could be a disastrous step. Remember that you do not always need to see the road ahead. It is sufficient, for the moment, to see Me.

When the time is right for a choice to be made you will know and I will assist you through it. Until that time be sure that merely keeping close to Me guarantees your moving in the right direction, despite questions and doubts raging in your mind.

– *John Woolley* [9]

A PRAYER OF ST IGNATIUS

When I copied this prayer into my journal, I was overwhelmed by the privilege of being hand-picked by God to serve him and to help to usher in his Kingdom.

> Eternal Lord,
> > King of all creation …
> > > I am moved by your grace
> > > > to offer myself to you
> > > > and your work.
> > I deeply desire to be with you
> > > in accepting all wrongs,
> > > > all abuse,
> > > > > all poverty –
> > > > > > actual and spiritual –
> > and I deliberately choose this
> > > if it is for your greater service
> > > and praise.
>
> If you,
> > my Lord and King,
> > > would so call
> > > > and choose me,
> > then take and receive me
> > > into such a way of life.

GOING WITH GOD

The road stretches out
        and as I take
        one step,
and two,
        the road moves on.
No end in sight.
        Just new
        horizons.
But you are there,
        taking the steps
        as I take them.
        Sharing
        the adventure.
Lord, it's risky,
there's so much space.
        But the
real shelter is not the
        walls I build.
It's in you.

— *Eddie Askew* [10]

I wrote this after meditating on the visit of the Magi and the phrase from the hymn: 'the gold of obedience'. Jesus himself seemed to be the model of obedience in that he took as his life's motto: 'I have come to do your will, O God.' I found myself wanting to echo that motto.

Grant, O Lord,
that I may be willing to go where you lead,
to endure hardships for the sake of your Kingdom,
to hold lightly to greatness or littleness.
And may my heart always prompt me
to seek your face
Beloved One.

— *LJH*

ANIMA CHRISTI

Soul of Christ, sanctify me
Body of Christ, save me
Blood of Christ, inebriate me
Water from the side of Christ, wash me
Passion of Christ, strengthen me
O good Jesus, hear me
Within your wounds hide me
Permit me not to be separated from Thee
From the wicked foe defend me
At the hour of my death call me
And bid me come to Thee
That with Thy saints I may praise thee
For ever and ever. Amen.

— *Anima Christi* [11]

UNBOUNDED LOVE

The next is my adaptation of a prayer of Charles Simeon. When I pray this prayer, I often have in mind one of the claims of Mary Euphrasia Pelletier: 'Our work is God's work, and God will protect it.' [12]

What is before us,
      we know not,
         whether we shall live or die;
but this we know,
         that all things are ordered and sure.
Everything is ordered,
         with unerring wisdom
         and unbounded love
         by You, our God,
You Who are love.
Grant us in all things
         to see Your hand;
         through Jesus Christ our Lord.

— *LJH*

HELP US TO BE GENEROUS

The Lord takes us,
    blesses, breaks
    and gives us.

Lord, help us to be generous as
    your bread broken,
    your wine poured out,
    your grain ground fine,
    your grapes trodden dry.

Tears, joy,
leavening, baking,
training, fermenting –
so much tender care

to make us
    light and nourishing,
    clear and stimulating,
    satisfying and delicious.

Lord, help us to be generous.

– *Winifred Brown* [13]

SHOW YOURSELF TO ME LORD

I wrote the prayer on the next page while meditating on Jesus's appearance
to Thomas while I was on retreat on St Thomas's Day 1995. The prayer was
inspired by Michael Cockett's song 'Show yourself to me, Lord'.

On this special day, Lord God,
I long to see you, as Thomas saw you:
              the love in your eyes,
                     the acceptance in your face,
                            the warmth of your smile.
My child, you said, if you would see me,
              gaze at my world,
                     look at my people,
                            reach out to my poor.

On this special day, dear Lord,
I long to hear you, as Thomas heard you:
              the kindness in your voice,
                     the invitation to draw near,
                            the lack of condemnation.
My child, you said, if you would hear me,
              hearken to the hungry,
                     listen to the poor,
                            hear the cries of those ravaged by war.

On this special day, dear Lord,
I long to touch you, as Thomas touched you.
              I long, lovingly, to finger your wounds,
                     to caress your feet,
                            to hold and be held.
My child, you said, if you would touch me,
              hold the hopeless,
                     reach out to the rejected,
                            nurse the sick in body, mind and spirit.
And rest assured that
inasmuch as you have seen, heard and touched my poor ones,
you have seen, heard and touched me.

                     – LJH

THE STRUGGLE

I once watched a fly fall off my bedside table into a spider's web and straight into the clutches of a spider. It reminded me of the way I am still ensnared by the seeming attractions of the world. Although the people I most admire are those who have given up everything for the sake of the Kingdom, I find myself longing sometimes for a more spacious house, a fixed salary rather than having to raise support, status (I don't like being an alien), a sense of belonging (Christianly and culturally), acceptance rather than suspicion (Secret Police). I envy those whose conscience allows them to serve Christ *and* live a comfortable, middle-class lifestyle! I sometimes feel that it's not fair! Such realisations gave rise to this prayer:

Jesus,
Beloved,
I feel as though a tug of war is going on inside me.
I feel drawn by you and your lifestyle
yet pulled away by the lure of riches and status,
honour and applause.
Give me the grace to say yes.

Father,
you didn't cling to your one and only Son,
You gave him up –
for me.
Enchant me over and over again
that my attachment to you
may loosen my grip
on life's seeming treasures
and set me free
to be the person
you always intended me to be.

– LJH

WE REST ON THEE

I first heard this prayer sung as a hymn on the film *Through Gates of Splendour* – the story of the martyrdom of missionaries who'd gone to work among the Auca Indians in South America. The film inspired me and the hymn haunted me. It was one of our wedding hymns. I echo it more and more as I go on in the Christian life.

'We rest on thee', our shield and our defender;
    We go not forth alone against the foe;
Strong in thy strength, safe in thy keeping tender
    'We rest on thee, and in thy name we go.'

Yea, 'in thy name', O Captain of salvation!
    In thy dear name, all other names above;
Jesus our righteousness, our sure foundation,
Our Prince of glory and our King of love.

'We go' in faith, our own great weakness feeling,
    And needing more each day thy grace to know;
Yet from our hearts a song of triumph pealing;
    'We rest on thee, and in thy name we go.'

'We rest on thee', our shield and our defender,
    Thine is the battle; thine shall be the praise
When passing through the gates of pearly splendour
    Victors, we rest, with thee through endless days.

– Edith Gilling Cherry, 1903

TAKE, LORD, AND RECEIVE

Take, Lord,
and receive all my liberty,
my memory, my understanding
and my entire will,
all that I have and possess.

You have given all to me,
to you, Lord, I return it.

All is yours;
do with it what you will.

Give me only your love
and your grace,
that is enough for me.

          – *From*
          The Spiritual Exercises of St Ignatius

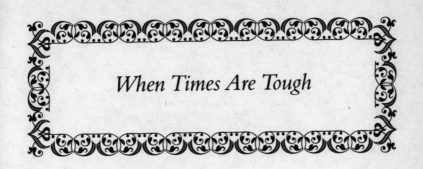

When Times Are Tough

To love God is to love the world.
To love God passionately is to love the world passionately.
To hope in God is to hope for the salvation of the world.

I often say to myself that ... God must feel very much alone: for is there anyone besides God who believes in the salvation of the world? God seeks among us sons and daughters who resemble him enough, who love the world enough that he could send them into the world to save it. [1]

So writes Louis Evely in *In the Christian Spirit*. But engaging with the world is not easy. Jesus warned that such service would be costly. 'In this world you will have trouble' (John 16:33). The disciples discovered the accuracy of this warning even while Jesus was with them: 'So many people were coming and going that they did not even have a chance to eat ... ' (Mark 6:31). After Jesus's death, problems assailed them at every twist and turn of the road as a glance at the Acts of the Apostles reminds us. In chapter 4, Peter and John are summoned and silenced by the Sanhedrin. In chapter 5, they are arrested by the Sadducees. In chapter 7, Stephen similarly is seized, harassed and stoned. Meanwhile, Saul is channelling all his energy and ingenuity into seeking to eliminate the infant church.

Recalling Stephen's martyrdom, Luke puts the situation graphically: 'On that day a great persecution broke out against the church at Jerusalem, and all except the apostles were scattered throughout Judaea and Samaria. Godly men buried Stephen and mourned deeply for him. But Saul began to destroy the church. Going from house to house, he dragged off men and women and put them in prison' (Acts 8:1–3). After his own amazing conversion to Christ, Paul also testifies to the truth of Jesus's prophecy: 'In the world you will have trouble' (John 16:33).

'I have been in prison ... and been exposed to death again and again. Five times I received from the Jews the forty lashes minus one. Three times I was beaten with rods, once I was stoned, three times I was shipwrecked, I spent a night and a day in the open sea ... I have been in danger from rivers, in danger from bandits, in danger from my own countrymen, in danger from Gentiles; in danger in the city, in danger in the country, in danger at sea; and in danger from false brothers. I have laboured and toiled and have often gone without sleep; I have known hunger and thirst and have often gone without food; I have been cold and naked. Besides everything else, I face daily the pressure of my concern for all the churches. Who is weak, and I do not feel weak? Who is led into sin, and I do not inwardly burn? ... In Damascus the governor under King Aretas had the city of the Damascenes guarded in order to arrest me. But I was lowered in a basket from a window in the wall and slipped through his hands.

- *2 Corinthians 11:23–33*

Yes. The cost of catching Christ's compassion for the world is incalculable. The mature, mellowed Peter puts it this way: 'Dear friends, do not be surprised at the painful trial you are suffering, as though something strange were happening to you. But rejoice that you participate in the sufferings of Christ, so that you may be overjoyed when his glory is revealed' (1 Pet. 4:12). Here, surely, the ageing apostle is building on the Beatitudes? In *Praying the Kingdom*, Charles Elliott suggests that, when we ponder these powerful sayings of Jesus, we replace the outmoded word, 'blessed' with, 'You are in the right place when ...

> You are in the right place when ...
>> you are poor in spirit
>> you mourn
>> you hunger and thirst for righteousness
>> you are merciful
>> you are persecuted
>> you become a peacemaker.

- *Matt. 5:1 ff*

Or, to use Eugene Peterson's punchy paraphrase:

> You're in the right place when ...
>> you're at the end of your rope
>> you've lost what is most dear to you
>> you've worked up a good appetite for God
>> you care

> you can show people how to co-operate instead of how to
> compete or fight
> when your commitment to God provokes persecution.2

My role, as I write, is to listen to, lead retreats for and pray for certain Christians who have chosen to live overseas – many of them living in the world's toughest places. I live overseas too. Although I live in a pleasant place, I frequently find the going tough. Loneliness often gnaws at my spirit. Stripped of the resources I took for granted in the homeland, helplessness often mocks me. The lack of language leaves me feeling a perpetual alien – a stranger in this place I now call 'home'. And yet I am curiously content. 'You sparkle', someone recently observed. I know that I am where God wants me to be for now. I know, too, that the pain and the frustration, the problems and the fears I face are but tiny hillocks compared with the mountain range of problems many of my friends face or have had to face in the past: some live in war-torn lands, some are locked in conflict with their colleagues, some lack the where-withal to live comfortably.

Most of the prayers that follow have been penned by such people: God's unsung heroes and heroines who have experiential knowledge of Jesus's warning: 'in the world you shall have trouble'. I wish every user of this book could meet the authors for themselves. Many of them are an inspiration – 'blessed' because, though the going is often very tough, they are in the right place for the right reason and they know it.

There are times, though, when even the most courageous of us feels like giving up. God knows this. At such times, so often, he speaks into our situation with sensitivity, pouring strength in where all strength seems to have evaporated. That is why, in this section, in particular, I make it plain that true prayer is two-way. We speak to God, God responds. Or God speaks to us and we respond.

RESCUED

I wrote this while reflecting on a car accident in which I was involved. The car was badly damaged but, by some miracle, I emerged unscratched.

> You, Lord, have been
> Light in my darkness,
> Hope in my despair,
> Love in my loneliness,
> the Protector who watched over me
>   when danger engulfed me,
> the Lifegiver who snatched me
>   from the jaws of death,
> the Intercessor who prayed
>   that my faith and resolve
>   might not fail,
> the Joy-giver who pierced and scattered
>   the dark clouds of oppression,
> my Security when the path before me
>   seemed like sinking sand.
> So my heart is ready,
> yes, my heart is ready
> to worship
> and adore
> You, the Holy One
>   to whom I may speak
>   as with a friend.

On the day I wrote this prayer I read the following in John Woolley's inspirational book *I Am With You*. [3]

You will be aware of much darkness, and of forces dedicated to obstructing your climb towards the heavenly sphere ... Love in creativity means that I am never remote from the inevitable heartaches of My children ... or, of course from *your* heart-ache.

Your sadness will be turned into joy.

— John 16:20

The agonising periods of existence, which would almost make you lose your hold on Me, can serve a very relevant purpose for you ... otherwise I would not permit them. Pain is the raw material from which you can be made a soul increasingly sensitive to My love's existence.

Life's pain and sorrows, allowed within My purposes of love are constantly used to create what is ultimately noble and strong and of the heavenly sphere: they thus give deeper meaning to the great miracle of existence itself ... the miracle that *I am*, and that this is a universe in which My love will triumph.

— John Woolley [4]

AT THE END OF MY TETHER

The prayer on the next four pages was written while I was still trying to work through the shock of a car accident. I turn to this prayer sometimes when I read of people being involved in road accidents. Although they emerge physically unharmed, the almost inevitable emotional trauma can create havoc for months.

Last night, Lord, I came to the end of my tether.
Four months of modern hassles finally wore me down.
The terror of travelling left my nerves frayed.
The frustration of communicating with people who neither act nor answer
persuaded me that I can no longer cope.
Discovering all the things we'd left behind left me disappointed,
despairing and angry.
The realisation that I won't now be seeing my family next month
gave rise to inconsolable grief.
Suddenly an inner dam burst.
Tears streamed relentlessly down my face,
tears that could not be controlled,
tears that flowed from a deeply damaged spirit.

I let them come,
they turned to sobs

My neck ached.
My back ached.
My hand ached.
Most of all my heart ached.

I sat under the stars
and wished I had died in the car crash.
My eyes drank in the majesty
but it could not touch my now bleeding heart.

I crawled back into bed
rather like that rat crept away to die,
and questions pestered me:
Is this what I have been called to do?
Why, why why ...

I called to you, Beloved.
Persistently,
Jesus, Je-sus, JE-SUS.
You didn't come,
at least, not in a felt way.
But I knew you understood.

I saw you stumbling along the Via Dolorosa,
unable to cope.
I saw you fall beneath the weight of the cross,
Or was it beneath the self-centredness of the world?
I heard you scream in Gethsemane:
'Father, take this cup from me now ...'
And I heard your fiat
        your Yes
        your:
        'Not my will
        but Yours
                be done.'

When I woke
you were there
beside me,
the tender One.
You held me in a memorable, momentary, motherly embrace.
I mourned that I'd left so many books behind:
'Read my other book,' you whispered.
The sunshine's slender fingers beckoned me out of my tent.
I parked my chair in a pool of sunlight.
The hard, parched, barren earth,
        the prickly pine needles,
        the liberal studding of stones,
        aptly summed up the state of my soul.
But before I could be ashamed
one autumn crocus captured my attention.
Its pale purple petals had parted in the sun.
It stood with palms upturned to the towering pine trees.
It revelled in the sun's rays.
Its openness revealed six sepals covered in pollen.
I gasped.
'My gift,' you whispered.
I gazed at this your gift.
You whispered again.
'Just as your eyes focus,
        not on the barrenness
        nor on the hardness
        of the terrain

but on the beauty before you –
the delicate delights of one small flower
that has pushed its way through many obstacles,
so my eye focuses
not on your failure
but on your desire
that your whole being
should be turned
to my honour and glory.
I honour you for that.
I hear your heartache and I care,
I see your exhaustion and I weep,
I discern that the gates of hell have been flung wide open,
That Satan has desired to have you that he might sift you
          like wheat.
But I am praying that your faith fail not,
that your resolve would be strengthened and not weakened,
that you would fix your gaze on me,
the Author and Finisher of your Faith-journey.
And I delight to hear that hymn
rising from the place of your woundedness:
'I know that, Redeemer God, you live
And that you will stand on the latter day
upon the earth
And though worms destroy this body
Yet in my flesh
I shall see God
My own beloved Redeemer God.'

So grant me the grace
to go on going on bearing hardships for the sake of the Gospel:
whether these hardships be the perplexities of the fast-changing
          world of
technology,
physical danger,
the attacks of the Evil One,
rejection,
loneliness,
superficiality,

the discouragement that comes through sowing precious seed in
        untilled soil,
or wherever.
Take me where you will.
Do with me what you will
Use me or not as you will.
I am yours.
You are mine.
That is the only certainty in this unsettled time.
It is enough.

– LJH

GOD'S LOVE WILL TRIUMPH

Life's pain and sorrows,
allowed within My purposes of love
are constantly used to create
what is ultimately noble and strong
and of the heavenly sphere:
they thus give deeper meaning
to the great miracle of existence itself ...
the miracle that *I am*,
and that this is a universe
in which My love will triumph.

– John Woolley [7]

WHAT IF ... ?

Many Christians working overseas find themselves in war zones or facing the threat of the outbreak of war. This prayer was written when waves of fear swept over me as I feared the worst.

Rumblings of war ...
What if we have to evacuate?
What if I have to leave my computer behind?
What if I have to abandon my books?
What if there's no time to say goodbye
to neighbours and friends?
What if ... ?

Worse.
What if there's no time to evacuate?
What if they forget to warn us
of the need to flee?
What if food supplies run out?
What if our home is invaded?
What if ... ?

Like those rumblings of war,
storm clouds gather over the mountain range this morning,
Lord,
a threatening, menacing, mass of steel grey.
Yet, already they're being dispersed by the rising sun
while those that remain are being tinged with pink and purple
on the underside.
'Whatever befalls, I'll be there,' you whisper,
'turning your grief to glory.'

My eyes turn from the sky to the soil.
There, perched on a tired-looking vine
sits a red-breasted robin,
singing full-throttle to herald the day.
'Look at the birds,' you whisper –
'especially when you are anxious.'

– LJH

I said, 'It is not good for man to be alone.' Yet, oh so many times I pull your friends from you, and you are painfully alone. Even surrounded by friends, you are an island and can only be talked to from distant shores. How often I have witnessed your heart crying, 'Oh friend, I cannot hold you close enough; you are still so very far away from me.'

That excruciating gap you must always sense, yet you are everlastingly trying to span it. You have learned that no arms will reach. I planted within you a homesickness for Me. I did this to keep you striving for Me. So many of you will exhaust yourselves trying to extinguish this flame of yearning with other hopeful fulfilments, while I stand by and watch you pass Me by.

Lonely heart, stop running, stop searching. Recognize the aloneness you feel, look at it truthfully, honestly, and courageously and lovingly. Admit your hopelessness in alleviating it. Recognize your inability to escape it. Then, in hope, not despair, lift that lonely heart to Me. Sometimes I will fill it with friends; sometimes with Me; sometimes, only with the full understanding that I know and understand; sometimes with not even that assurance. Sometimes I will fill it with My absence.

Your inner being may passionately crave the heart of a fellow human being to talk to, to understand, and I may not grant what you ask. But I will give you the understanding of faith to believe that I'm aware of your loneliness, knowing that it is not time to dry your tears. Sometimes time must evaporate them. If a friend were to wipe them away too soon, you might not grow as I have planned for you. Let My awareness of what you suffer now in loneliness be your companion. Offer it to Me ... I can use it to shape you! You, watch with Me in Gethsemane ... let the others sleep. With Me, understand loneliness; with Me, listen; with Me, be healed.

— *Joan Hutson* [5]

THIS IS IT

On 2 October 1991, after a series of incidents that could be called psychological harassment on the part of Sendero, and not long after the killing of
two authority figures by them in a section of our parish in Lima, a quarter of
an hour's walk from our house, we were wakened at midnight by very loud
banging on our door. In the light of previous happenings we presumed
Sendero had come for us! The landlord called out to them and they said
they wanted the Priest, and the landlord told them to go to the Parish. On
reflection we decided it was another tactic of psychological harassment –
very effective.

> This is it. It's them. They're at our door.
> There's no escape. There's no going out.
> Just wait for the moment.
>
> I see the shadows on the glass.
> I hear the loud knocking again.
> I feel the need for protection.
> I experience fear in the face of possible death.
> In the dark I seek something to cover me
>   to protect my vulnerability.
> And something outside of me to make God present to me
>   my cross, my rosary, something tangible
> of God with me in the 'hour of our death'.
>
> Relief, in the sound of the landlord's step.
> Relief, in their responses to his question.
> Relief, in the sight of disappearing shadows.
> Relief, in the sisterly sharing of the moment.
>
> God in the Fear.
> God in the Relief.
> God in the Sharing.
> 'My hour had not yet come.'

>   – *Barbara Cameron,*
>   *Arequipa, Peru,*
>   *10 December 1991*

DISPLACED PERSONS

On 3 October 1991 we left our place in Canto Grande, Lima, the day after
the knocking on the door at midnight, although we had already discerned and
reached a decision to leave for a safer area. I felt the experience let me feel
some of the emotions the people feel when they have to leave their area or
their country because of the risk to their lives if they stay. I felt, too, that I
experienced some of their feelings as they try to settle somewhere else.

Departing quickly. Hurried goodbyes.
   Packing only essentials. Leaving
      things behind.
         Sympathized with. Misunderstood.
           From the permanent, to the
            temporary.
              From danger, to safety.
                From what was ours, to
                  what is theirs.
                    Reproachful eyes.
                      Welcome hearts.

Repeated questions. Repeated
   explanations.
      Approval from some. Judgement from
         others.
           Dependent on the kindness of
            others.
              Anxious not to be a nuisance.
              Unfinished endings. New
              beginnings.
                Delayed reaction
                  to tension, to grief.

Living in some small way, another
   aspect of solidarity
with the displaced persons in our city,
   in our world.

'Make your home in me.'

                           – *Barbara Cameron*

PSALM 63

Two weeks after the incident that led us to leave Canto Grande (after weeks
of tension from psychological harassment on the part of Sendero Luminosa,
who had a strong presence in the Pueblo Joven, the poorer area where we
lived on the outskirts of Lima), a delayed reaction to the tension left me
feeling very fragile and feeling God's absence (possibly because of some un-
conscious anger towards God because of all the violence in Peru in these last
few months). But the experience of God's absence has stirred up a longing
for him in some more tangible way in my life at this time.

'God you are my God, I am seeking you ...'
But you're the God-in-hiding.
It's difficult for me to find you,
especially in the violence.

'My soul is thirsting for you ...'
for your kingdom of justice and peace.
Those who thirst for justice will have
their fill
but you didn't say when, Lord. How
much longer?

'My flesh is longing for you ...'
for the warmth of your touch midst the
cold news of more killings,
for the tangible light of your love in
the darkness,
for the healing peace of your presence
in the pain.

'You have always helped me ...'
I want to be able to sing again for joy
in the shadow of your wings
but the joy eludes me.
I want to be able to cling close to you
but you seem so distant I can't
feel you close.

I want your right hand to support me.
I need to feel that support. Why
can't I?

'God, you are my God, I am seeking
you.'

— *Barbara Cameron*

IN DARKNESS

In all those dark moments, O God, grant that I may understand
that it is you who are painfully parting the fibres of my being in
order to penetrate to the very marrow of my substance ...

— *Teilhard de Chardin* [8]

THE GOD-IN-HIDING

Something of depression or 'the dark night'. Part of my delayed reaction to the violence, and the circumstances surrounding our exodus from Canto Grande, Lima, was to experience the absence of God very strongly, which was painful. It seemed like all the sources I'd usually nourished my faith from had dried up. All, that is, but two, the Word I'd find in Scripture that continued to be life-giving, and in moments shared with the sick I was accompanying, discovering faith or hope or love or all three in the midst of suffering.

> I used to find Him in prayer
> > but could not hear him then.
> I used to find Him in Eucharist
> > but could not touch him then.
> I used to find Him in Reconciliation
> > but could not feel His healing then.
> I used to find Him around me
> > but could not see Him then.
> I used to find Him in music
> > but could not play it then.
>
> I looked for Him in the violence
> > but He was hidden from me.
> I looked for Him in Faith
> > but it was hard to believe.
> I looked for Him in joy
> > but joy was a stranger to me.
>
> Where could I find this God-in-Hiding?
> > Unconsciously; I sought Him in my
> > sick brothers and sisters
> > and in them He revealed
> > Himself to me.
>
> Faithfully, I sought Him in His Word,
> > and in the darkness, the light of
> > His Word could not be
> > overshadowed.

— *Barbara Cameron*

A PRAYER IN SUFFERING

Dear Lord and Saviour, Jesus Christ,
I hold up all my weakness to your strength,
my failure to your faithfulness,
my sinfulness to your perfection,
my loneliness to your compassion,
my little pains to your great agony on the Cross.

I pray that you will cleanse me,
       strengthen me,
            GUIDE ME,
so that in all ways my life may be lived
as you would have it lived,
without cowardice,
and for you alone.
Show me how to live in true humility,
      true contrition
         and true love.

> — *Found on a prayer card*
> *with the initials M.S.*

KEEP YOUR HAND IN MINE

You know that all the qualities you see in Me
are available to you ...
Be sure that your hand is firmly in Mine ...
I know that in your heart
is that longing to know Me more perfectly.
I honour that longing,
and that is why you are sure of My patience
in all your sufferings.

> — *John Woolley* [9]

'As the Father has loved me ... so I
have loved you ...'

I believe you, Lord, but in this moment
I don't know that love.
I want it, need it to heal my soul,
long to feel the warmth of it.
Where is it? Why can't I feel it?
When I most need to.

'So that my own joy may be in you ...
and your joy be complete ...'

If you wanted your joy for me, Lord,
why does it elude me now?
Why is my spirit joyless? My body
needs to know the healing power
of the joy of your Spirit. Share with
me again that joy that I may know joy
and my joy may be complete.

'I call you friends ...'

It's your friendship, Lord, that gives
my life meaning, but it's painful now
to feel so cold and cut off from you.
I need to feel the warmth of your
friendship, I need some tangible sign
of it, I need you to share with me
again all you learned from the
Father, I need you to listen to me, to
be there for me in the chaos around me.

'The Father will give you anything you
ask in my name ...'

I've been asking for the miracle of
peace, but I need a miracle for me,
Lord. I ask the Father in your name
for a lasting experience of your love
that will bring with it the joy of
your Spirit. In that love and joy I
will know your friendship again. I
will hear you call me friend and be
able to respond in love as friend.

— *Barbara Cameron*

LIGHT OF THE WORLD

The next prayer was written as a result of meditating on the raising of
Lazarus. In my imagination I had 'become' Lazarus — still wrapped in the
grave clothes. As people were removing those restricting cloths, I became
conscious of a blinding light penetrating the darkness, flooding the dark
tomb with light, showing me how to mount the steps so that I could reach
Jesus. The Light of the World stood, at the top of the stairs, resplendent in
glory.

Dear Light of the World,
Your radiance pierces the gloom of the tomb,
　　　　penetrates the darkness of my bewilderment
　　　　and so floods my path
　　　　　　　that I stride with joyful confidence
　　　　　　　　　towards you,
　　　　　　　　　　　my Resurrection and my Life.
May your light guide me when my path is dim,
breathe authoritative life into me when I feel full of fear,
and draw me ever closer to you —
　　　　Holy Trinity,
　　　　Three yet One,
　　　　One yet Three,
Ever-blessed circle of Love.
　　　　　　　— *LJH*

Loving heart, every pulsation of your heart courses My blood and yours throughout your body. Sadly I have watched some of this precious nourishment ebb away because there is a break in your heart. You kept your heart so openly vulnerable, so unguarded, so woundable to everyone. Then, not an alien, not a stranger, but your closest friend broke it. Not keenly and swiftly with words, but joggedly and slowly with unexplained indifference.

Weakened by the loss of blood, you realized more than ever your dependence on Me. The more you called, the richer became My transfusions to you. Now that more of My blood than yours flows through you, I want to heal that broken heart – the blood that is dwindling from the break could nourish other souls rather than aimlessly river through the sands of time.

In My eternal now, I reach back and instantly heal the break. You are serving My purposes without knowing it, by responding to My healing touch and believing that your world is unfolding according to My universal plans. There may remain in your heart that 'why, why' that began so many years ago when your fragile, open heart was broken. But with that incessant 'why' will come the understanding that 'all things work together unto good for those who truly love Me.'

When you see what the loving willingness to remain in painful darkness until My light lets you see the 'why' achieves, you will say, 'Break my heart, again, and again, and again. The more of Your blood that You transfuse, the more I become You and the less I remain me. I can bear the 'why' and take comfort in your one non-committal response! Just because!'

– *Joan Hutson* [10]

WHEN DEPRESSED

You, O Christ,
who were despised and rejected by men,
know how I feel when,
by fault or failure,
or from sheer exhaustion,
I am cast into lonely pits of depression.
Draw me up from such despair
on the thin
yet cable-strong rope of prayer
to stand on 'this great roundabout –
the world'
and praise you.

> – *My adaptation of a prayer of*
> *William Cowper, 'The Jackdaw'* [11]

We would pray this morning, our Father, about our fears:

fear of unpleasant confrontations in the suqs★;
fear of traffic accidents where we will be judged guilty irrespective
of our innocence;
fear of not finding a job back in our homeland when our term here
is finished;
fear of what may happen to members of our families absent from us;
fear that our presence here is, in the long run, meaningless;
fear that we made a mistake when we came here;
or fear that we came here for the wrong reason;
fear that we will not get our exit visas on time.

We know that perfect love casts out fear;
fill our lives this day with that perfect love
that we may be honest in coming to you with our fears
and that we may allow your love to drive our fears away.

Help us, Lord, to find joy in daily life around us:
in the warmth of a quiet conversation with a friend;
in the unexpected blessing of discovering a kindred spirit in a new
friend;
in a friendly wild cat eager for affection;
in the giggling little Arab girl as she stares out of a taxi window;
in a fresh insight into a long-remembered verse of Scripture;
in a new-found ability to trust you where we had always held back;
in the calming of our anger when we discover the historical roots of
the reasons why the people around us act and think the way
they do that so infuriates us;
in the peace that comes to us when we remember to pray.

Bless us, Lord, in our needs.
Bless us in the loneliness that sweeps over us far from the
hills of home.
Bless us in the agony of loneliness separated from
family.

— *Professor Kenneth Bailey* [12]

★ suqs: bazaars, market places

A PRAYER FOR THOSE WHO ARE AFRAID (2)

Written for and prayed at a Graduation ceremony in Beirut, Lebanon in 1968.

O Thou who art hidden behind the curtain of sense,
    incomprehensible in Thy greatness,
    mysterious in Thine almighty power;
O omnipresent One, beneath whose all-seeing eye our mortal lives
    are passing,
    be present in our service tonight as we seek Thy
    special blessing on these Thy servants.

O Thou who didst walk the tiring trails of Judaea and Galilee,
    give strength to Thy servants here tonight as they begin
    their journey.
O Thou who didst search out the lonely places to renew Thy spirit,
    renew the spirits of these thy disciples.
O Thou who didst preach release to the captive and hope for the
    oppressed,
    give compassion to Thy servants that they may not be
    trapped by callousness and indifference.
O Thou who didst live and preach the gospel in all of its shattering
    clarity,
    make straight our paths that we might lead and not mislead
    the faithful.
O Thou who didst teach all men to know Thy love,
    inspire us to know and proclaim Thy love in our
    love-hungry world.

Cleanse this night these Thy servants as they pass this milestone in
    their pilgrimage.
    Burn out of them and us all selfish ambition,
    all self-seeking,
    all eagerness to seek first the praise of people.
Purge them of all desire to show themselves as morally superior to
    other people,
    of all eagerness to hide evil behind a mask of saintliness,
    of all inclination to preach in order to impress.

Deliver them, O Lord, from all paralyzing fears:
    fear of the uncertainty of their future;

fear of lack of daily bread;

fear of life in the unsettled work in which they are called
to serve;

fear of personal inadequacy before an awesome task;

fear of losing touch with Thy empowering Spirit;

fear of losing the assurance of Thy presence to guide on
life's path;

fear of an inadequate faith for the temptations on the way.

Give them, O Lord,
of Thy Spirit,
of Thy Resurrection power,
of Thy unfailing grace

that they may not go up like a rocket and come down like a dead stick;

that they may not rely on what they have learned
and become a tired and broken record in their preaching
and teaching;

that they may not be crushed by spiritual loneliness in isolated
assignments;

that they may not fossilize in spirit and offer only a copy of someone
else's obedience.

Give them, O Lord, of Thy Spirit that they may

be illuminated by the light that the darkness could not
overcome;

that they may be filled with truth and certainty in our
uncertain world;

that they may be able to provide answers for honest seekers
and raise questions for dishonest seekers;

that they may be voices ringing with the truth of Thy gospel;

stakes driven into the shifting sands of our times;

and steady lanterns in the windy night.

Deliver them from the fear of people that they may truly fear Thee.

Help them to find the place of service where they can give most
fully of themselves in Thy service.

Be Thou their guide,

O Thou who are the Way, the Truth and the Life.

In Christ's name we pray. Amen.

— Professor Kenneth Bailey

A PRAYER FOR THOSE WHO ARE AFRAID (3)

Professor Kenneth Bailey wrote this prayer for a group of Christians who used to work and worship together overseas. I often use this prayer when praying for such people because it captures so well some of the stress factors they encounter.

O Lord,
we are all your disciples;
we are all your servants, your ministers.
We have come here from classroom, office, home, student desk, hospital ward, committee meeting, consultation room, library and shop.
>   Through the week we have tried to be the ministers of the
>   church, fulfilling as faithfully as we can the callings to
>   which you have called us.
Well – not quite – there are those moments when we failed;
>   when we were short-tempered –
>   unable to see an interruption as an opportunity;
>   when our hope dimmed and there were flashes of anxiety
>   over the future –
>   a future that we know is in your hands – and thus secure.
But we have already told you that we come in weakness seeking
>   forgiveness
and that forgiveness we have here received.

So now, Lord, here we would lay afresh our ministries at your feet.
>   At times we are caught up in drudgery – so give us patience.
>   At times we wonder if the task is really worth it – so give us
the long view that sees beyond the frustration of the moment.
>   At times we question whether we have really heard your
>   voice clearly.
>   We wonder whether we are fulfilling the real task to which
you would call us.
>   So remind us of the paths of discipleship we have walked
>   thus far
>   that have brought us to where we are.
>   At times we see only church employees as ministers and
>   ourselves as something less;
>   so help us see again that every bush is a burning bush
>   and let us see its light and be warmed by its fire and

be amazed afresh that it is not consumed.
Give us eagerness to turn aside to see this great sight,
for there God speaks uniquely to us.
We have another problem, Lord;
we carry out our discipleship in a secular and alien society –
a society that does not share many of our deepest and most precious loyalties.
So we have built walls and live our lives in compartments in order to survive.
We know that you did not do this when your Word became flesh and dwelt among us.
We seek the same transparency that all those who saw Jesus of Nazareth witnessed in his words of life.
Help us to tear down those walls and discover the liberating force of this same
openness and vulnerability.

So send us back to our ministries, Lord, as your disciples.
For we have come here to remember who we are and to be strengthened to fulfil
those ministries to which you have called us.
Grant us your Holy Spirit that we might know the quiet power that was so evident in the life of our Lord.
We pray this in his name.
Amen.

– *Professor Kenneth Bailey*

WAITING FOR GOD

Professor Kenneth Bailey again gives us a glimpse of some of the struggles
faced by Christians working overseas.

'I waited patiently for the Lord;
    He inclined unto me and heard my request.'

We know that the Psalmist sings such things, at least when he is
    feeling good.
Sometimes we feel that way too.
        Then there are other times when the sky is as brass above us
        and the earth is as iron under us;
and we cannot see the cloud the size of a man's hand rising
    over the sea.
So today,
we do not come in strength, but in weakness to be made strong:
not in wisdom, but in ignorance that we might learn your wisdom;
not in the fullness of your Spirit, but in emptiness to be filled.

We have seen your light shining brightly in the dark of night.
Its warmth and illumination have enriched us.
If it were not so, we would not have come to this place.
But you have called us to be a city on the hill.
        It is safer in the house, and quieter, and all there are friends.
The city on the hill is too exposed, Lord, and we are afraid:
        afraid that we will have to speak up, and will not know what to
        say;
        afraid that we will be identified and some harm will come to us;
        afraid that the things we hold most dearly will be subject to
        mockery.
So – we fail to be a city set on a hill.
        We are more like lamps flickering in the wind.
        Deliver us from fear of the wind;
        deliver us from retreating back into the house;
        deliver us from fear lest our light go out –
                for you have kindled it and if we trust, we know it will
                shine through any storm.

'I waited for the Lord.'

Lord, we waited for your advent – and rejoiced in the light that
came into the world in a manger.
We anticipated your Cross and hoped for the Resurrection –
and found meaning in pain and hope in new life.
Now we await the coming of your Spirit.
Fill our lamps that we may with confidence shine in whatever place
you send us: in office, store, market, study, home,
classroom, hospital and city streets.
We pray for all those who seek peace and justice in this beloved,
troubled land.
We pray for its leaders that they may have wisdom from above for
all the daily decisions that they must make.
Bless us in the week ahead that we may take each new disruption as
an opportunity to seek new doors of ministry.
Fill our lamps, Lord, with the oil of your Spirit.
For only in your light do we see light
and without your Spirit, darkness descends upon us.

– Professor Kenneth Bailey

I AM

I was regretting the past and fearing
    the future.
Suddenly, my Lord was speaking:
MY NAME IS I AM.
He paused. I waited. He continued.
'When you live in the past,
    with its mistakes and regrets,
        it is hard.
            I am not there.
My name is not I WAS.
When you live in the future,
    with its problems and fears,
        it is hard.
            I am not there.
My name is not I WILL BE.
When you live in this moment,
    it is not hard.
        I am here.
            My name is I AM.'

           – *Helen Mallicoat, source untraced*

Going Where It Hurts

Going Where It Hurts

LISTEN

Listen my children:
listen to me.

I would speak to ears
    that will listen to me;
I would speak to eyes
    that will see as I see;
I would speak to lips
    that will say the words I give;
I would speak to minds
    that will seek to think as I think;
I would speak to hands
    that will be my compassion to the world;
I would speak to feet
    that will walk where I want to go;
I would speak to hearts
    that will beat only to love me.

Listen my children:
listen.

I speak from a war-torn country
    where brother fights brother;
I speak from the anguish of a young mother
    whose baby has been taken from her;
I speak in the old man hanging on to life
    by a thread;
I speak in the young woman for whose illness
    medicine has no cure;
I speak in the troubled heart,
    the mind filled with fear;

I speak in the howling of the wind,
the thunder in the sky,
the crash of a hurricane ...
but I speak too in the rainbow;
in soft dewdrops;
in shafts of sunlight;
in stillness.
I speak in laughter;
I speak in a smile;
but most of all my children,
I speak in silence.
So listen my children –
listen to me;
listen – listen ...

– *Sue Ashdown*

If we do what those words beg us to do, if we step off the treadmill from time to time, seek solitude and open the ears of our hearts to God, we will hear many voices. We may tune in to God's voice that finds a myriad ways of whispering the healing message we all need to hear: 'I love you.' We will also almost certainly hear the plaintive cry of the sick and the sorrowful, the lonely, the depressed and the oppressed. We can't go to them all. Neither is that our calling. We can go to some. We can pray for others.

In the still place Sue Ashdown describes, God will fill us afresh with his love so that, when we go to his hurting ones, we will not go empty-handed, we will go with eyes full of his love, lips that speak words of wisdom, consolation or grace, hands and arms that express his tenderness and warmth.

And, of course, when we go, we visit, not only a human hurting person, we meet and touch Jesus himself. As he reminds us, in Eugene Peterson's paraphrase:

When the Son of Man takes his place on his glorious throne ... all the nations will be arranged before him and he will sort the people out, much as a shepherd sorts out sheep and goats, putting sheep to his right and goats to his left.

Then the King will say to those on his right, 'Enter, you who are blessed by my Father! Take what's coming to you in this kingdom. It's been ready for you since the world's foundation. And here's why:

> I was hungry and you fed me,
> I was thirsty and you gave me a drink,
> I was homeless and you gave me a room,
> I was shivering and you gave me clothes,
> I was sick and you stopped to visit,
> I was in prison and you came to me.'

Then those 'sheep' are going to say, 'Master, what are you talking about? When did we ever see you hungry and feed you, thirsty and give you a drink? And when did we ever see you sick or in prison and come to you?' Then the King will say, 'I'm telling you the solemn truth: *Whenever you did one of these things to someone overlooked or ignored, that was me – you did it to me.'*

– Matt. 25:31–40 [1]

Sometimes, when we visit those who are hurting, we will neither know what to say, what to do or how to pray. At such times, it can be a strange comfort simply to remind ourselves that God knows. As Sue Ashdown puts it, God 'knows each grain of sand, each blade of grass, each ant and spider that walks unseen by human eyes. God knows each breath we take, each thought we think – before we think it (Ps. 139:2)'. 'Even the hairs on our heads are numbered' (Luke 12:7a).

HE KNOWS

A leaf falls to the ground:
a tiny flutter,
no sound.
    He knows.

A sparrow sheds a feather:
the slightest movement,
no noise.
    He knows.

A tiny spider curls and dies:
no trumpet call,
just nothing.
    He knows.

A lily bends and breaks in the wind:
no scream of pain;
just silence.
    He knows.

A heart lifted in joy:
but whom to tell,
just a smile.
    He knows.

A mind torn with pain:
only silence is heard,
no heart's cry.
    He knows.

A hand lifted in defence:
no justice felt,
just vulnerability.
    He knows.

A soul seeking to follow:
no perfection here,
just sin.
    He knows.

A life longing to serve:
No unhindered walk,
but stumbling.
  He knows.

A breath drawn in waiting:
no certainty for ease,
just obedience.
  He knows.

A whisper from heart's depths:
no eloquent phrases,
just 'My Lord'.
  He knows.
  He knows.

      — Sue Ashdown

AN INSTRUMENT OF PEACE

Lord, make me an instrument of thy peace.
Where there is hatred, let me sow love.
Where there is injury, pardon.
Where there is discord, vision.
Where there is doubt, faith.
Where there is despair, hope.
Where there is darkness, light.
Where there is sadness, joy.
O divine Master,
grant that I may not so much seek to be consoled as to console;
to be understood as to understand;
to be loved, as to love;
for it is in giving that we receive,
it is in pardoning that we are pardoned,
and it is in dying that we are born to eternal life.

      — Source unknown.
      Attributed to St Francis of Assisi
      1181–1226

AN INDIAN GIRL

Some time ago a poor young Indian girl lay seriously ill in a Calcutta hospital. She knew that she was not likely to recover, but she was not afraid. One afternoon she had lain quite still, with her eyes shut, and for so long that the nurse came to see if she was all right. The girl opened her eyes. Had she been asleep? asked the nurse. 'No,' said the girl, 'I was praying.' 'What were you asking God for, to make you well?' asked the nurse. 'No, I wasn't asking for anything. I was just loving him.'

'It is in such quiet, deep communion with God,' wrote Phillip Loyd, then Bishop of Nasik, 'that spiritual forces beyond our reckoning or comprehension are released. They can be released in and through us, if we will only draw near to him prepared, expectant, waiting to love him.'

– Quoted in John Carden [2]

WHO COULD HAVE KNOWN

Children are a gift from God and they give incredible joy – they also bring unspeakable sorrow. In J. Neville Ward's book *Five for Sorrow, Ten for Joy* [3] he writes of how Mary and Joseph 'lost' Jesus when he was twelve years old. They found him three days later in the temple, but he returned to them a different person no longer needing them in the same way. They had to let their child 'die' – to let him become a different person, changed, adult, free to love them without staying emotionally dependent on them. This 'letting go', this 'losing' can be frighteningly painful to parents. Most mothers of teenagers who are in the midst of those much-dreaded adolescent years can identify with Mary's pain and, I believe, could have written the following.

Often I've been given the privilege of praying for parents in pain. At such times, I sometimes use this prayer. I have also been given a burden for the homeless children of Nepal who have been brought up to 'earn a living' by picking pockets. I sometimes use a derivation of this prayer as I pray for them and for their parents.

Who could have known
    as I held that longed-for,
dreamt-of,
    suffered-for,
tiny
    'bundle of joy' close to my heart
that later
    she
would break it?

Who would have known
    that after all the joy,
the closeness,
    the oneness,
the watching,
    the holding,
the loving,
    would come
the anguish?

From heart's depths,
    from very roots of being
cries a voice
    rent with pain,
torn with the longings of love:
    a single cry
in desperation:
    'Help her – help me …'

Who could have known?

I have loved so much,
    planned so much,
longed so much,
    been one with.

Now part of myself
    is dying;

longing stretches out
        with arms to hold
and stays
        empty
as the cry comes again:
        'Help her – help me …'

Who could have known?

And from nowhere,
        from everywhere,
from deep to deep
        comes with longing –
gently,
        lovingly,
God.

'I knew.
I have loved so,
planned so;
I am one with
My arms of love
hold her
hold you.

I knew
I know.

        Come.'

                    – *Sue Ashdown*

PARENTS IN PAIN

Father, my beautiful child
suffers –
she champions you
among her fellows
without compromise,
but it's her
they cull out,
cut down
and skin alive.

Once
I fought her battles for her;
I'm helpless now.
Such courage
makes me proud –
but when she bleeds,
I haemorrhage;
her rejection
aches in my spirit,
her loneliness
sobs in my heart,
and prayer is pain.

'Daughter,
I hear you.
My beautiful child
was crucified too.
His suffering
broke my heart.'

'This my Son whom I love ... hated without reason.'

– *Linnet Hinton* [4]

MY CHILD HAS GONE

Sue Ashdown writes: 'Friendship is about communication and forgiveness
... In the case of our children, as they become young adults, it's also about
two loving arms which never close in rejection but only round the new-
found friend our child has become.'

She's gone, Lord.
The child I once knew –
and in her place – a woman
vulnerable – as all women are –
lacking polish,
needing assurance perhaps,
but nevertheless
a woman.

The pain of her birth into womanhood
was every bit as great
as the pain of her birth,
the more so perhaps, because of its
suddenness –
then months of waiting,
of preparation.
Now – in a day –
separation.
She's gone.

My innocent daughter,
now initiated
into all the rites of womanhood
which by their very nature meant
I was not there.
Without me
her voyage of discovery
was begun.
She's gone –
and I must let her go.
Time now for painful rebuilding –

where innocence – now knowledge;
where wondering – now certainty;
where hesitancy – now assurance;
where childlike trust
now I must accept –
a woman's vulnerability.

Viewpoints considered – decisions made
– without me;
ideas formulated – carefully;
girlhood pushed back
– womanhood embraced
as she steps from my arms –
into his.
But she will discover
that womanhood's freedom is incomplete
and she may need my arms again.

So I will wait.
Not in desperation – but patiently,
for she may need me yet
as man needs man
and woman needs another woman –
and we will walk together, she and I
side by side.
For my child is gone
and in her place –
a woman.

Lord, give me the grace to wait.

– *Sue Ashdown*

A WEDDING DAY

Weddings can be hard for clergy wives. While other couples enjoy one another's presence, the clergy wife often sits alone. If her marriage is going through a time of turbulence, or if she is depressed for any reason, the wedding service can trigger the kind of pain being expressed by the clergy wife who breathed this prayer.

I sit alone.
Alone! Alone! Alone!
Mocked by the ceremony about to begin,
'It is not good for man to be alone,'
said God.
And here I sit
alone.
I see couples cuddling,
laughing,
loving into each other's eyes.
They smile across the pews at me
alone,
pitiably, pitifully alone.
A few tears
squeeze from the beggar's bowl
of my aching heart,
as those words of peace
slice through my soul
with the precision of a butcher's knife.
Once *we* made those vows.
But still I sit
alone.

'Marriage is a mosaic'
claims the preacher.
A mosaic.
My imagination plays with the image.
In offering one another the fragments that remain;
in placing one another, bit by bit,
on the ready plaster of God's love
he makes us new.

Carefully he selects that which is offered,
piecing us together, bit by bit,
making us one.

'But tell them of the pain'
my heart cries.
Fragments are broken pieces.
You must offer little pieces of yourself
if you would form a good mosaic.
Tell them that the joins show –
ugly, dirty, unsightly seams
that unite the coloured pieces
holding them together,
making of two persons, and many fragments
one whole.

Tell them that it hurts
to be broken so small
to contribute to the picture.
Tell them that Love
like a plastic frame
holds their two loves together for always.
Tell them that when all hopes are dashed
into tiny, tiny pieces,
when all illusions explode
like an untimely bomb,
when their union lies in tatters
wasted on the ground,
he comes.
Patient.
Tender.
Skilful.
To gather up the fragments that remain,
to make of them a new picture –
one whole.

Lord, press me,
press us,
our few remaining fragments
into the cement of your love
that we, too, may live
and hope
and love again.
Two 'I's
but one 'We'.

– *Anonymous*

A WOMEN'S LOCK-UP WARD

Reflecting on a visit to the women's lock-up ward at a psychiatric hospital.

What breaks the people's hearts?
What tears their minds apart?
What is it that has the power
to reduce the creation in the image
        of the divine God
into a twisted heap of pain?

How is the human spirit healed?
How is the shattered mind restored?
        How is the power released
        that can free God's image
in the twisted heap of pain?

        Can I be that power Lord?
        Can I love as you loved?
        Touch as you touched?
Can I restore that which you created
        to what you created it to be?

        Make me your instrument Lord,
        hollow me and blow through me
the music that heals.

– *Zita O'Neill*

LETTING GO

Sometimes, I find, the depth of my concern for a person can become an
obstacle to my own prayer for that person. I have therefore found this a
powerful and moving prayer to pray for some of the precious people in my
life. I like the emphasis on letting God be God!

To a dear one about whom I have been concerned.

I behold the Christ in you.
I place you lovingly in the care of the Father.
I release you from my anxiety and concern.
I let go of my possessive hold on you.
I am willing to free you to follow the dictates
       of your indwelling Lord.
I am willing to free you to live your life
       according to your best light
       and understanding.
Husband, wife, child, friend –
I no longer try to force my ideas on you,
       my ways on you.
I lift my thoughts above you, above the personal level.
I see you as God sees you, a spiritual being,
       created in His image, and endowed with
       qualities and abilities that make you
       needed and important – not only to me
       but to God and His larger plan.
I do not bind you. I no longer believe that you
       do not have the understanding you need
       in order to meet life.
I bless you,
       I have faith in you,
          I behold Jesus in you.

– *Author unknown*

GOD'S MIGRANTS

Linnet Hinton recalls that she wrote this prayer as a result of meeting in the home of Fijian Indians. 'We ... represented a wide divergence of races and cultures. Two things united us: our common insecurity as new migrants and our shared love for the Lord Jesus Christ. Some had suffered persecution. As a recent arrival to Australia myself, I felt an enormous kinship with these special people who are so often disregarded by society.'

> They flee to us for refuge
> from violent storms
> of persecution, famine and war;
> leaves stripped from their trees,
> scattered by hurricanes of hatred and fear.
> But you, Lord God, are master of the wind,
> you ride upon the storm.
> Not one of them is lost.
>
> What they were before they are no more –
> men of substance and repute perhaps,
> now nobody – unrecognized, undervalued,
> strangers in the world, struggling to survive
> a painful transplant into foreign soil.
> But these aliens, Lord,
> are your chosen ones,
> hand-picked to follow you through suffering –
> sprinkled with your blood,
> sanctified by your Spirit,
> people of destiny,
> whom the world does not know
> and is not worthy.
>
> Thank you, Lord, for blowing them our way.
> They may come empty-handed,
> but their hearts are full of indestructible treasure,
> true trophy of triumph in trial –
> the knowledge of God.
> They found you in fear-fuelled furnaces,
> walked with you through death-dark valleys.
> You were the one reality when all else dissolved –

the living God.
They knew you and were changed.

What stories they tell!
We warm our cold spirits at the fire of their faith
and reach out to touch you again.
Through this timely transfusion of costly new blood
you heal our anaemia, restore our energy
and bring fresh hope to a sick society.
O God, keep them from drifting
into a self-centred search for security
that would drain their vitality,
wither their witness and snuff out the light.
For they are your good gift to us
and we need them
desperately.

'God's elect, strangers in the world ... scattered ...
 chosen ... of God.'

– Linnet Hinton [5]

FOR THE AFFLICTED

We bring before you, O Lord,
the troubles and perils of people and nations,
the sighing of prisoners and captives,
the sorrows of the bereaved,
the necessities of strangers,
the helplessness of the weak,
the despondency of the weary,
the failing powers of the aged.
O Lord, draw near to each
and show me how I may draw near
in your Name,
for the glory of Jesus.

– My adaptation of a prayer of
St Anselm, Archbishop of Canterbury
1033–1109

DOES ANYBODY CARE?

Linnet Hinton explains how she came to write this prayer. 'When this cruelly abused girl came to me for help, I felt helpless, out of my depth. Her condition challenged not only my love but my confidence in the ability of the Lord Jesus to salvage her.'

She sat there,
a spent shell –
empty voice speaking
of unspeakable things done to her,

At 20, disintegrating,
loosely labelled 'schizophrenic',
the fragments of her once three-dimensional self
laid out deadly flat,
glued and greyed with drugs.
Afraid to live, afraid to die.

Another casualty of a callous consumer society
where plastic people exist
to be used and abused for perverted pleasure,
factory-made duplicates –
anonymous, disposable.

But she is not bio-degradable, nor recyclable,
finally absorbed by Mother Nature
into harmless oblivion.
Her soul is human, eternal,
hand-crafted, individual,
designed with infinite potential for good – or ill.

A life blighted in bud
by high-tech barbarians
unable to appreciate the delicacy of divine artistry,
or the priceless blood of purity.
Employing violence, pressure-packed,
these vandals deface innocence with ugly graffiti
and viciously violate vulnerable virginity.

The city streets are littered
with social flotsam and jetsam such as she.
Garbage dumps of modernity,
heaped high with human waste,
lie at the very threshold of hell
where demonic cultures gather
to shred whatever's left of hope and sanity
and pick the bones to bare despair.

Does anybody care?

The question hangs in the fetid air.
I see him stooping there, bleeding hands
searching patiently through the wreckage –
the Scavenger of Souls.
My heart is full of tears,
love and faith fight selfish fears.
What use am I?
He turns and bids me bring my bit of salvage to him –
one treasured soul, a lost and lonely girl.

'Jesus is able to save completely those who come
to God through him ...'

– *Linnet Hinton*

GOD OF THE WHOLE WORLD

John Carden writes: 'You find them near almost any bus station in small-town Pakistan. Pathetic little booths where, in front of an antiquated box camera, and against a painted backdrop of mock Moghul palaces, domes, turrets, terraces, flashing streams and strutting peacocks, a man may have his photograph taken. Thus he temporarily perpetuates the illusion of grandeur, before returning once more to dust-coloured dullness of the real life which normally surrounds him.'

> God of the whole world,
>   forgive us the little booths of our
>   own creation,
>   forgive us the limiting of our concern,
>   the artificial backcloths of our
>   denominationalism,
>   forgive us our make-believe, our sense of
>   self-importance, our posturing on our
>   small enclosed stages,
>   and lead us out yourself into a world
>   in which every single happening is of interest
>   to you, and every single creature
>   of value in your sight.
>   — *John Carden* [6]

INSTANT PEOPLE

John Carden writes: 'Whether it be instant coffee or cake, packaged soup or mashed potatoes, or even instant insurance out of a machine at an airport – these things have become commonplace to many of us. In Pakistan, however, the only thing that is really instant is the presence of people. All 130 million of them. Not the ones you really want to be instant, like the electrician when the light has failed, or the plumber when the flush is leaking, or the carpenter when the house is falling down, or the shop salesman when you want to buy something ... These are never instant. But the people who are always instant are the onlookers ... You can't escape from people in Pakistan. Here people are instant, and urgent.'

I often use this prayer when I pray for the world's poor and for those who have sacrificed everything to go and work with them. To be constantly 'gawked at' can feel demoralising and irritating and does not create a comfortable back-cloth for ministry.

> O God,
> forgive us our packaged and
> plentiful food
> and give us a responsible concern for the
> instant poor.
>
> – *LJH*

LOVE FOR GOD'S PEOPLE

This prayer was inspired when the author suddenly saw, through an archway, a single white minaret set in a sea of sky blue and almost perfectly framed in the deep arch in which he and his family stood. The archway thronged with holiday crowds that day that gave birth to this compassionate prayer.)

> God guide the people of Pakistan
> at work and at prayer,
> at ease, and in disease.
> And by wise teachers and good leaders
> bring her many people to the gate
> of that Kingdom
> where the sudden sight of your beauty
> will dull all pain,
> wipe away all tears,
> heal all wounds,
> quicken all consciences,
> and draw from people everywhere the response:
> *through Jesus Christ our Lord!*
>
> – *John Carden* [7]

BALL OF FIRE

John Carden explains: '"But a ball is a thing to play with," exclaimed our younger son when, waxing poetic, we had described our May sun setting as "a great ball of fire". You might say that out here it is the sun that plays *with us,* forces us into our dark rooms and behind our dark glasses, under fans and showers. On to our beds in the afternoons for what one foreigner has described as a "lovely dull time." ... But ... there are times, sleeping out under the stars, eating hot-weather fruit (melons and mangoes), relaxing in the garden at 10 o'clock at night with cool drinks and friends, and the perfume of the night blossoming shrubs, when you begin to think that living here is quite fun.'

> For fans,
> iced water
> and cool night breezes,
> we praise your name, O Lord.

>   – *John Carden* [8]

MY GOD, I'M HOT

John Carden writes: 'In the West, people soon start to complain if the temperature soars to 30 degrees or so. In Pakistan, as in other countries, Christians from the West find themselves working in temperatures of 47 or more – energy-sapping and something you never seem to get used to. Hence the prayer opposite:

My God, I'm hot.
Sweat trickles down everywhere,
clothes hang damp and crumpled,
eyes close so soon after waking,
feet are tired and swollen,
tempers are short,
rooms are dark, heavy, blanketed in heat,
water is in short supply and is ever
lukewarm,
arms stick to tables and saturate writing paper.
My God, I'm hot.
But each drop of sweat, every temptation to irritation,
help me to offer to you,
and on behalf of those who have no
possibility of escape from the burden of this
heat –
the chronically sick,
the elderly,
fever-ridden, pale children,
the mother who waves the hand-fan and
brushes off the flies,
the father who waits his turn in the queue
for water, or is sent heavy-hearted for a
white sheet and a string of jasmine
blossoms, for the funeral;
my God, unite my present unspeakably
trivial discomfort to the blood and sweat of
Jesus, on behalf of this perverse and
unforgettable land and its needy people. Amen.

– *John Carden* [9]

THAT HATEFUL SOUND

John Carden explains: 'At certain times of year – September in particular – listening for the sound of the evening flight and going to the airport to see departing friends becomes almost as much a part of our Christian lives as going to church. And when you go *there* on the following Sunday, the gaps in familiar family groups still further accentuate the reality of the loss.'

I have often watched such goodbyes at airports in the Two-thirds World. There is something peculiarly painful about such farewells somehow. The phrase 'for good' sums up the pain. I often think of this prayer when working in the Gulf and in other countries where it is customary for married men and women from a variety of countries to live and work away from their families to earn money to send home. Such people need a great deal of cherishing and understanding as do their loved ones left behind. (LJH)

> There it goes, Lord,
> just on the 17.20 hours they talk about
> at airports, and that new, universal,
> jet-style language,
> so far removed
> from the slowly rising and setting sun
> and the pattern of time Pakistan keeps in
> other departments of her more leisurely life.
>
> But *here* there can be no delay as,
> heavy with hope,
> the plane laboriously pulls itself up over the
> heat of Lahore
> en route for Karachi
> to catch westward-bound flights tonight
> and tomorrow morning, early.
> And what is it toward which they go, Lord,
> those up there?
> The present moment's ease concealing
> days and weeks and
> months of negotiation; delays,
> letters, endless footing from office to office

for passports, injections, no–objection
certificates,
visas, state-bank permits, income-
tax clearance; until
finally the looked-for hour has arrived
of hand-shakes, garlanding, bear-hugs,
and proud glances,
the unease as between men and women,
husbands and wives even,
possessing no reserves of experience
to meet this situation,
walking together to the last barrier, the only
two or three steps of privacy
permitted for one, two, three,
four, five years, or for good.

And down below at the airport, the plane
out of sight now,
the crowd thinning out,
making their way home by car or taxi, or even,
more mundanely,
waiting at the bus stop (for no single class
has the monopoly on air travel, these days).
Hands that carried garlands, string-marked,
still smelling of flowers, or
clutching empty boxes that but a few minutes
ago held hearts of silver tinsel,
their owners returning to houses bereft
tonight of a father, a husband, or a son,
but filled with pride, and talk of the travellers,
and the hope of an early return.

— *John Carden* [10]

IRENE

Barbara Cameron explains: 'Irene was killed by the terrorist group Sendero Luminosa, on 21 May 1991. The reason given was her involvement with the distribution of food to the poorer people. The one who shot her was said to be a 16-year-old girl. The funeral was a deeply moving experience. (I use this prayer when I pray for Christians working in difficult, seemingly impossible circumstances because they have responded to the call of God to go, to love, to incarnate his love.'

Irene's been shot. Dead? Jesus …
Her crime? Giving food to the hungry.
I was hungry and you gave me to eat.
Life, how cheap, how fragile.
Victim of the abuse of power,
powerless.

What message for life, this death?
What new call to be heard?

In the midst of violence
a presence of peace.
In the face of death
promoters of life.
In community unity
challenging disunity.
Reflecting on life, grateful,
receptive,
listening, accompanying, incarnating.
Living justly.
Loving tenderly.
Walking humbly with our God, with His
people.

Contemplative missionaries.

— Barbara Cameron

POWERLESSNESS

Barbara Cameron reflecting on her first two years in Peru. It is a
prayer/reflection that many of us who work overseas could echo, a prayer that
those working at home could adapt and pray on our behalf. But working
with the powerless brings its own rewards as the following reflections reveal.

Powerless in the face of sickness,
of painful, unnecessary, expensive sickness
of baby, of child, of mother, of youth,
undermining the quality of life, causing premature
death.

Powerless in the face of poverty,
of degrading, dehumanising poverty
that makes beggars of the young, the old,
the handicapped, the sick.

Powerless in the face of strikes,
of recurring, indefinite, crippling strikes
affecting the sick, the poor,
cutting links with family and friends.

Powerless in the face of transport,
of unreliable, insufficient, overcrowded transport
that may or may not run at the scheduled time,
that may or may not follow the scheduled route.

Powerless in the face of bureaucracy,
of red tape, form-filling, power-happy bureaucracy
demanding so much of your time and energy
and patience and money.

Powerless in the face of language,
of fast-flowing, softly-spoken, poorly-enunciated
language, resulting in not-knowing, misunderstanding
or isolation, in difficulties in communicating.

It is the experience of the 'little people'
in the world of today,
those without health or money or education
or work or status or mobility,
those who haven't a voice,
victims of systems, of history, of politics,
of the abuse of power.
Christ knew powerlessness
in His birth, in His death.

May my experience of powerlessness
lead me to a more real solidarity
with the 'little ones' of this world,
to a deeper compassion,
to a liberating humility
that will open me to receive
from those whose lives touch mine,
that will enrich the quality of my presence
to those who come into my life.

— Barbara Cameron

'Hermanita' you called me
and I did feel small
in so many ways.

Small and helpless
in the face of your helplessness,
with your legs that refused to move,
your sores that wouldn't heal.

Small and powerless
in the hospital system
with insufficient funds, technology and staffing
to improve the quality of your young life.

Small and in awe
of your ability to joke and laugh,
to rise above the frustration
in spite of the pain.

Small and humbled
by the trust you placed in me,
the confidences you shared,
the tears you shed.

Thank you for inviting me into your life, Irene,
as your 'Hermanita'

             — Barbara Cameron

*Hermanita' means 'little sister'

ROSARIO 14

Always there in your wordless world,
Aabandoned ... condemned
to spend your years
in a hospital bed
dependent on whoever came by
to meet your needs.

So little – so much
to give
by way of your smile.

Somehow your smile communicated
what we all need to hear:
acceptance, welcome,
a reason to hope
when there's no reason to hope.
Gracias,
Rosario.

                     – *Barbara Cameron, Peru 1989*

THE GOD WHO CARES

On flying from Delhi to Bombay:

By train this journey takes twenty-four hours.
It can be hot, dusty, noisy, crowded.
But this way it gives me less than one hundred minutes of air-
conditioned ease in
a soft seat, with refreshments served on the way.
Far below are circles of green on the brown plain –
fields watered by patient irrigation.
Each patch with its cluster of houses in the centre.
And the villages are linked by long roads
where the slow ox-carts travel.

The country is so great,
too vast for any one man to know.
Yet each yard of road is known to someone or other,
every green square the fruit of someone's toil,
every least house has someone who calls it 'home'.
Only to you, Lord, is it all known perfectly.
No green patch, no foot of road, no toiling man is outside of your care,
your knowledge or your love.
I kneel in spirit, and adore
a God great enough at once to see the whole
and to know intimately every smallest part.

> – *Marjorie Prior,*
> *CMS Mission Partner* [11]

NO BEAUTIFUL THOUGHTS

Sometimes the person in need is one's self. We might then need to pray a prayer asking for help:

No 'beautiful thoughts' today Lord,
 just an overwhelming sense
 of failure in this situation,
 of helplessness,
 of inadequacy,
 a sense of being totally unable
 to handle it
 alone.
Come in Lord Jesus and make something
 of this miserable heap.

– Sue Ashdown

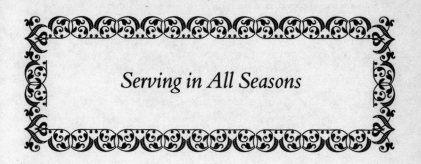

Serving in All Seasons

Serving in All Seasons

The sea ebbs and flows. The moon waxes and wanes. The sun rises and sets. The seasons come and go drawing us into nature's rhythm of life. The church, too, woos us into its own rhythm: Advent moves into Christmas. Christmas is followed by Lent. Lent resolves into the crescendo of Easter. After Easter comes the Ascension followed by Pentecost and so on. For the person of prayer, each of these seasons of the spirit presents a particular challenge. Advent, that season of watching and waiting, begs us to re-affirm the Lordship of the Christ who came, the Christ who still comes, the Christ who will come again.

Christmas, the season when we celebrate Christ's first coming, presents us with such a medley of models of self-sacrifice that thoughtful, prayerful Christians find themselves full of desire to emulate the example of Mary and Joseph, the shepherds and the magi, Simeon and Anna. Christmas and Epiphany turn into times of re-dedication which, in itself, is a preparation for Lent.

The six-week run-up to Easter that we call Lent can become the springtime of the soul for those who observe it well. Although the soul may have seemed as gnarled and dead as the bare branches of fruit trees in winter, by Holy Week the fruit of the Spirit may have begun to bud again. Watching with Christ in Gethsemane, staying with him as he hangs on the Cross, entering into the emptiness of Holy Saturday and marvelling at the mystery of his Resurrection can be to the soul what warm sunshine is to tight-shut buds – part of the nurture they need to burst into blossom before maturing into full fruitfulness.

The prayers in this section revel in the church's seasons and show how, for some people, special days have become landmarks of commitment on the pilgrimage of faith.

ADVENT (I)

Still at last, dear Lord,
     I come to you
weary from the busyness of a thousand things
     that clamour for attention
but longing to feel your touch afresh
     this Christmastime.
Kindle in me
a love that finds time for you,
that responds to you,
that yearns for your return.
Cause my heart to leap for joy
as I anticipate that great fact of the future –
     your re-entry to earth.
Pour into me the certainty that believes
     that all life is to be lived under the shadow
       of that miraculous return,
the courage to live life your way,
and the resilience to hold on to that hope
     when times are hard
       or the body tired.
Bring me to Christmas Day
     not irritated with Christmas commercialised
but rather rejoicing in the message of the angels:
     to ME
       this day
         is born
         MY SAVIOUR.

– *LJH*

ADVENT (2)

O Lord,
my years grow long
and my time short.
Let me make haste with my repentance
and bow both my head and heart.
Let me not stay one day from amendment
lest I stay too long.
Let me cease without delay
to love my own mischief
and to abandon, without a backward look
the unfruitful works of darkness.
Lord, grant me new watchfulness
to lay hold upon opportunity for good.
Make me at last put on the whole armour of light.
Rank me among them who work for their Lord,
loins girded, lamps burning
till the night shall pass
and the true light shine.
Let me sing the new song,
following the lamb whithersoever he goes,
loving wheresoever he loves,
doing whatsoever he biddeth,
until the perfect day,
the day of the true Advent
when the light comes into the world
for ever and ever.

– *Eric Milner-White* [1]

ADVENT (3)

God, keep me steadfast in faith,
      make me joyful in hope,
          and untiring in love.
            Now
            and always.
               Amen.

– *LJH: adaptation of a blessing for
the first Sunday of Advent* [2]

CHRIST'S SECOND COMING

Lord Jesus Christ,
Sometimes, I close my eyes and try to imagine
    what it will be like
when you come again – in glory.
Will the sky blush, as with the sunrise?
Or will it glow as at sunset?
Or will your glory pierce through the clouds
    in a sudden blaze of light?
Who can tell?
And who can tell how that grand reunion
    with loved ones
        will take place?
Amid all these imponderables,
    I cherish the certainty
that when you come to take us home
our loved ones who loved you while they were on earth
    will be with you.
And we shall be with you
in that place where death has lost its sting,
where goodbyes cease,
where there is no more parting
    from those we love
        or from you.

– LJH

HE'S COMING BACK

Sometimes, Lord,
it seems too good to be true
that you really are coming back
to take us to be with yourself.
At other times, I confess,
life here on earth seems so good
that I don't want you to come back –
at least, not yet.
Forgive my coldness.
Forgive my doubting.
Fill me afresh with awe
        this Advent
as I anticipate your return
        and heed your command
                to wait in readiness.
Give me the grace
        to change my attitude
                and my lifestyle
so that your coming,
        whenever you come,
                may find me
                        greeting you with joy,
                                heartfelt thanksgiving
and an eagerness
        to drop everything instantly
                to be with you
                        FOR EVER.

– LJH

PREPARING FOR CHRISTMAS

Such a flurry of excitement
        seemed to fill the air
                in town today, Lord.
Women hurried through the bazaar
        clutching poinsettias
                and Christmas cakes
                        and tinsel to hang on Christmas trees.
Men puffed and panted and heaved and sighed
        as they persuaded huge evergreens
                    into their pre-Christmas show-places –
                        outside offices and shops and public
                        buildings.
Father Christmas appeared, too
        as though from nowhere
                still clutching his customary dove,
                    still gazing at the fairy lights that straddle the
                    streets
                        and twinkle above the shoppers.

I became a part of the euphoria, Lord.
I also clutched my poinsettia
        and tinsel,
                pine cones sprayed with silver,
                red candles
                    and scarlet ribbons.

'But what are they celebrating?' I wonder.
What am I?
You came.
You continue to come.
You will come again.
That's it in a nutshell.
That's the cause of *my* celebration
or, as one small boy put it:
'Dear God,
Most people like Christmas because of the presents.
I like Christmas because it's your birthday.' [3]

                        – *LJH*

CHRIST'S BIRTHDAY

As we await your birthday, dear Lord,
give us a glimpse of the mystery
        of the incarnation.
Cause us to wonder that you,
        the Creator of the universe,
peeled off the splendour and glory
        of the heavenly places
and put on the form of a foetus
        in a woman's womb.
Restore to us
        the ability to stop,
        to ponder,
        to marvel
        at you,
        the radiance of God's glory,
        the flawless expression of the divine nature,
        at God made man,
        God in human form,
        God asking to be touched
                        and handled
                        seen
                        known
                        loved .
And teach us to love you without inhibition
that this Christmas
the glow in our hearts
may bring joy to you
and warm the lives
of those less fortunate.

— *LJH*

NOTHING IMPOSSIBLE

The miracle you did for Zechariah and Elizabeth, O God,
boosts my ability to believe in you,
reminds me that the age of miracles is still not past,
and prompts me to marvel at the way
      you intervene in people's lives today.
This Christmas, miracle-working God,
    remove from my eyes the scales of unbelief,
    take from me the heart of stone that refuses to yield to you,
    prepare me so that I am ready to receive you
      with awe and wonder,
      joy and thanksgiving
      and grateful love
      that flows through me to others.

– LJH

LIKE MARY

This prayer was inspired while I was contemplating the arrival of the Magi on one occasion. As I prayed, I sensed that, as the visitors from the East entered the humble home where the Holy Family were living, Mary immediately drew their attention away from herself and on to her child. 'Don't look at me – look at him,' she seemed to say.

    Father,
    be with me as I seek to find the right balance
    between going out and coming in.
    And may my motto always be,
    'Don't look at me, look at Jesus.'

– LJH

THE ROAD TO BETHLEHEM

'O tell us please' the Wise Men asked,
'Which is the way to Bethlehem?'
And men have sought it ever since
To find the way to Bethlehem.

Here twinkle all the bright lit shops;
Are they the stars of Bethlehem?
And churches stand with pretty cribs;
Are these the paths to Bethlehem?
Now travel agents sell their flights
That daily land near Bethlehem.
Should we take train and plane and bus
And so will come to Bethlehem?

But some there are that know the way,
The only way to Bethlehem,
And those are they that we should ask
To find the way to Bethlehem.

'You need to travel down and down,
Who seek the road to Bethlehem,
Past all the outward worldly ways
That do not lead to Bethlehem.

Down to the deep centre of your hearts,
To find the road to Bethlehem,
Where your own love can welcome Christ,
This is the way to Bethlehem.'

— *Peter Marshall:*
source not traced

GAZING ON GOD

Mary gazed on God,
    held God,
        gave God to the world.
           Hallelujah.

How can I, Beloved,
    cherish you,
        gaze on you,
           give you to the world?

Yes.
You've told us.
By cherishing the poor and the sick,
the hungry and the imprisoned,
the lost and the lonely,
we are cherishing you.
As I ponder these mysteries
and thus gaze on you,
give me the grace to take you
into the world –
to my neighbours,
my friends,
in particular,
    to those working in the world's tough places.

– LJH

LIKE THE SHEPHERDS

This Christmas, dear Lord,
like the shepherds,
I would bow in awed wonder
before the majesty of heaven
revealed in the form of a baby.
Fill me afresh with love
        as I contemplate the mystery.
Reveal yourself to me so that
        like the shepherds
        and the angels
        my heart may be filled with joy.
And transform me so that
        I may become more and more like
        this Christ-child I worship:
        ready to do your will
        in everything,
        even at cost to myself.

– LJH

A SAVIOUR

To *you* is born a Saviour

Holy child,
I take you into my arms,
hold you,
gaze on you,
love
and adore you.
And the realisation dawns that
contemplating you
and serving you
is the antidote to temptation.
I realise, too, that the reason why you came
was to deal with the wayward streak in me
that would so quickly serve self.
To me this day is born my Saviour.
This is mystery.
This is Love –
unearned, undeserved, Love.
My heart desires to return to this loved place often,
to hold and be held,
to cherish and be cherished,
to serve and be served,
to love and be loved,
that I may carry the fruit of this loving
to those who do not know that to them
a Saviour has been born.

– *LJH*

HOLY CHILD

Holy Child,
when I turn to you
and hold you
all other loves pale into insignificance.
For this,
I thank you.

Holy Father,
you have given this child
to deal with my waywardness.
For this I give you
humble, heartfelt praise.

Holy Spirit,
so work in the hidden parts of me
that my whole being may be turned to the worship and service
of the Beloved
who deigns to be seen
           and heard
               and touched
                 and held
                   by me.

           – *LJH*

CHILD OF MY LOVE

The reason why I came into the world was because
I saw the human predicament –
your predicament.
And I loved you.
So I gave my Body for you.
It was my pleasure to do this for you,
dear child of my love –
a privilege entrusted to me
by my Father.
And now it rejoices my heart when I see you
receiving me,
relishing my life-giving sacrifice,
savouring my love.
Come often,
for although the threads of the web
in which you are held
have been broken,
you are not yet completely free.
My life and my death,
my Body and my Blood
can set you free
increasingly.
So come,
child of my Love.
A mother pines for her child
when the child seems far away from her.
That is but a pale reflection
of the emptiness I feel
when you seem far away from me.
So come often,
come well.
Let no other loves lure you
up life's cul-de-sacs.
Only stay on the path I show you.
When its going is rough
be assured that I will be with you.
Even when you do not feel my presence by your side.

Child of my love
I am yours
and you are mine
for ever.

– *LJH*

PRAYERS FOR THE NEW YEAR

Jesus, the Name high over all
In earth and heaven and sky
Angels and men before him fall
And devils fear and fly.

Jesus, the Name that charms our fears
That bids our sorrows cease
'Tis music in the sinner's ears
And life and health and peace.

Oh! That the world might taste and see
The triumphs of his grace
The arms of love that compass me
Would all mankind embrace.

Happy if with my latest breath
I might but gasp his Name
Preach him to all and cry in death
Behold the Lamb.

– *Charles Wesley, 1707–88*

I said to the man who stood at the gate of the year: 'Give me a
light that I may tread safely into the unknown.' And he replied:
'Go out into the darkness and put your hand into the hand of God,
that shall be to you better than light and safer than a known way.'

– *Minnie Louise Haskins*

THE NAMING OF JESUS

'On the eighth day, when it was time to circumcise him, he was named Jesus, the name the angel had given him before he had been conceived' (Luke 2:21). While meditating on Jesus's circumcision and naming on one occasion, I wrote the following prayer:

Lord Jesus, as I embark on yet another year
and with this reminder
        of your supreme sacrifice
rising before my eyes,
I give you myself afresh.
Take me as I am.
Take me where you will.
Do with me what you will,
this New Year
and always.

        – *LJH*

As this New Year unfolds, O God,
enlarge my vision of yourself,
deepen my trust in your love,
increase my faith in the perfection of your purposes
that when you speak
I may listen,
and when you direct
I may obey,
confident that you will never
        cause your child
                a needless tear.
        – *LJH*

LIKE ANNA

Lord Jesus, I would worship you as Anna did,
in spirit and in truth.
Like her I would
submit all my nature to you,
that my conscience may be quickened by your holiness,
my mind nourished by your truth,
my imagination purified by your beauty,
my will surrendered to your purpose,
my heart opened to your love.
Like Anna
may I turn myself to you
in selfless adoration and ceaseless love and praise.

> *– LJH: adaptation of a prayer of*
> *George Appleton*

EPIPHANY

You prompted the Magi
              to abandon their plans, Lord,
to return to their homes
              via a different route.
We, too, have known that prompting
              as you implanted in us
                    the desire to abandon our well-laid
plans
                          for yours.
Beckon us both afresh,
              though we may see no reassuring
                    guiding star.
Make unmistakably plain
              the path you would have us tread.

> *– LJH*

LIKE SIMEON

This prayer was inspired by meditating on Simeon's stillness and effectiveness. The Gospels only make one mention of him and, so far as we know, he only met Jesus once and yet his name goes down in history as one who worshipped with his life as well as his lips.

I desire to be like Simeon, Lord.
So still before you
    that I can hear
        and respond to
            every prompting of your Spirit.
So in tune with you
    that I may become
        a sensitive, loving mouthpiece
          for you.

I yearn, too, to become like Mary,
    ready to have her heart pierced through
        as by a sword.
But I'm more than a little scared
    and know there will be times when I will rescind this
        prayer.
So give me your grace
    to remain open to you
        and open to others.

As this new year unfolds,
    grant me the quiet trust
        that watches
          and waits,
            that listens
              and believes
in you
    at all times
        and in all places.

— *LJH*

EPIPHANY

I sat watching the candles
burning beside the stable
this evening, dear Lord.
One, in particular, drew me to itself.
Its flame was so bright,
so straight,
so pleasing.
'I want to be like that FOR YOU',
I whispered.
Through Isaiah, you promised:
'I will make you a light to the nations.'
Thank you.

> – *LJH:*
> *biblical reference is Isaiah 49:6*

LIGHT OF THE WORLD

Light of the world,
you shine into my darkness.
You have become
      my Rescuer and
      my Saviour.
Shine your inextinguishable light
      into every nook and cranny
        of my life,
and may that light beam through me
      to others.

> – *LJH*

Make me
a still place of light,
a still place of love
of You.
Your light radiating,
your love vibrating,
your touch and your healing
far flung and near,
to the myriads caught
in darkness, in sickness,
in lostness, in fear.

Make a heart-centre here
Light of the world.

— *From a prayer card produced by*
West Malling Abbey, Kent, UK

PRAYERS FOR PALM SUNDAY

These two prayers were inspired by meditating on the role the donkey played on the first Palm Sunday. In my meditation, I 'became' the donkey and found it a profoundly moving experience.

> Holy Spirit,
> create in me more and more
> the desire to decrease
> so that Jesus might increase.
> Give me the strength to plod on –
> through crowds,
> through criticism,
> and through crises
> that Christ may be proclaimed and known
> through who I am
> as well as what I say and do.
>
> – *LJH*

> Eternal King,
> reign in me – in every part of me.
> Use me as you used that donkey
> to carry you
> and your message
> into the capital,
> to cleanse
> and to heal. Amen.
>
> – *LJH*

RIDE ON, RIDE ON IN MAJESTY!

Ride on, ride on in majesty!
Hark all the tribes 'Hosanna' cry;
O Saviour meek, pursue thy road
With palms and scattered garments strowed.

Ride on, ride on in majesty!
In lowly pomp ride on to die;
O Christ, Thy triumphs now begin
O'er captive death and conquered sin.

Ride on, ride on in majesty!
The angel armies of the sky
Look down with sad and wondering eyes
To see the approaching sacrifice.

Ride on, ride on in majesty!
The last and fiercest strife is nigh;
The Father on His sapphire throne
Awaits His own anointed Son.

Ride on, ride on in majesty!
In lowly pomp ride on to die;
Bow Thy meek head to mortal pain,
Then take, O God, Thy power, and reign.

— *Henry Hart Milman, 1791–1868*

O make me understand it,
help me to take it in,
what it meant to Thee, the Holy One
to bear away my sin.

— *Katherine A. M. Kelly*

HOLY WEEK

At the beginning of this Holy Week, dear Lord,
I would reaffirm your Lordship.
Take the reins and lead me
    where you will.
Take everything I have
    and everything I am
        and do with me what you will.
May my life glorify your name,
    now and always.
        – LJH

FOR ME (I)

St Ignatius used to encourage his retreatants to meditate on the fact that
Jesus's suffering and death was 'for me'. I attempt to do that regularly which
is why several of the prayers in this section contain the recurring phrase: For
me. This first prayer was written while I was meditating on Jesus's trial before the Sanhedrin.

Silent, Suffering Saviour,
I stand at the brazier,
warm myself by its glow,
see you across the crowded courtyard,
and feel helpless,
powerless.
With my eyes,
with my face
I communicate the love I feel,
the support I long to give.
But you have gone beyond the place
where any mortal can help you now.
And you're there
in that condemned place
because you love me.
You are suffering like this
FOR ME.
        – LJH

JESUS BEFORE PILATE

Written when meditating on Pilate's question:'Are you a King?'

Creator of the world,
shine the torch-light of your truth
into the nooks and crannies of my life.
Show up any inconsistencies and hypocrisies in me
that you would eradicate.
Bring every part of my life into alignment with yourself,
for you are *my* King.
I want you to reign over me
for ever and ever,
for your glory,
for my wholeness,
and for the extension of your Kingdom.

— *LJH*

BEFORE THE CROSS (I)

Written as a result of contemplating the soldiers as they hammer the nails
into Jesus's hands and feet.

'You can't do it'! I cry.
Yet they hammer the nails into his sacred hands.
They do it FOR ME.

I weep.

Lying prostrate on the floor,
my body forming the shape of a cross,
I hear his cry:
Father, forgive …
I give him my life.
I give him my love.
Total surrender.

— *LJH*

THE FLOGGING

Flogged,
thorn-crowned,
mocked,
spat upon
FOR ME.

Battered,
bruised,
despised,
disabled
FOR ME.

Beloved,
you have given so much for me,
give me the grace to go on and on
pouring out my life-blood for you,
counting the cost
but continuing to give and give
like you.

– LJH

FOR ME (2)

The prayer overleaf was written as a result of meditating on the Fall, from Genesis 3, that prompted me to recall the miracle of salvation and served to remind me that Jesus died for me. I record in my journal: 'At the end of that meditation and through supper, it was as though a fire burned inside me. I longed, felt desperate, to discover how I could help in God's Rescue Operation of a sin-sick world.' Hence, the use of Frances Ridley Havergal's words from the hymn 'Take my life and let it be'.

Father,

I am almost lost for words.
That you should sacrifice your Son *for me*
fills me again with deep, deep gratitude.
Awed.
Speechless.
Sobered.
Surrendered.

How can I withhold anything from you?

I've felt the effects of the medicine of your salvation:
how deeply healing it is
this side of eternity
let alone the next.

In the light of such love, my Lord,
there are no words,
only one offering is adequate –
the offering of myself.
So:
Take my life and let it be
consecrated, Lord, to Thee
take my moments and my days,
let them flow in ceaseless praise.

– *LJH*

LET MY HEART CRACK

O Lord, Holy Father, show us what kind of man it is who is hanging for our sakes on the cross, whose suffering causes the rocks themselves to crack and crumble with compassion, whose death brings the dead back to life.

Let my heart crack and crumble at the sight of him. Let my soul break apart with compassion for his suffering. Let it be shattered with grief at my sins for which he dies. And finally let it be softened with devoted love for him. Amen.

> – *A prayer of the Franciscan Bonaventure,*
> *thirteenth century*

BEFORE THE CROSS (2)

For drawing me to yourself, I praise you, O God.
For your tender, life-changing love, I worship you.
For the power of your blood to change my sin from scarlet
to snow-white I adore you,
because the only reason for this transformation
is that you loved me enough to die for me.
I feel drops of blood falling
from your beloved wounds
on to my hands, my head, my heart,
intermingling with my blood,
making me clean.
For the wonder of this powerful detergent
I give you humble and heartfelt thanks.

> – *LJH*

TREE OF CALVARY

O Tree of Calvary,
send thy roots deep down
into my heart.
Gather together the soil of my heart,
the sands of my fickleness,
the stones of my stubbornness,
the mud of my desires,
bind them all together.
O Tree of Calvary,
interlace them with thy strong roots,
entwine them with the network
of thy love.

— *Chandran Devansen* [4]

Today he who hung the earth upon the waters
    is hung upon the Cross.
He who is King of the angels is arrayed in a crown of
    thorns.
He who wraps the heaven in clouds
    is wrapped in the purple of mockery.
He who in Jordan set Adam free receives blows
    upon his face.
The Bridegroom of the Church is transfixed with nails.
The Son of the Virgin is pierced with a spear.
We worship you, Lord Jesus Christ.
Draw us to yourself with bands of love.
Show us the glory of your Resurrection.

— *My adaptation of*
    'Hymns of Good Friday' [5]

ONLY LOVE

Lord
I come to You
in the silence of eternity.
I have no words –
only love.
I can hardly bear to look at You
for Your love is enormous
and mine is so small.
But the silence is too noisy Lord,
I hardly dare to breathe –
still the silence,
silence the stillness Father
– for there is movement yet.
I close my eyes and look at You,
my Father, my Lord, my Love.
You reach out and hold.
I feel the nails
and as Your crown of thorns
 – my crown of thorns –
pierces Your head
 – my head –
my eyes weep tears of pain
and my heart bleeds tears of love.
And in that tiny, timeless moment of oneness
all my heart can do is to whisper
        'Father, I am here'
and across eternity
I hear You whisper back
        'Child, so am I.'
                    – *Sue Ashdown*

SHEPHERD AND STAR

The following was written on 31 October 1992, and given to me personally
as a prophetic word.

No one could be crucified in my place.
Even though Simon helped to carry my cross to Calvary,
he was not nailed on it when we reached there.
And my mother could not take my place;
she could only watch my agony and weep for my pain.

But Simon had his place in my sacrifice,
and my mother had her special role of com-passion.
And I call men and women in every age
to re-present my passion,
and to act as channels of my life
to those who are searching for me.

It is neither success nor power that will attract them,
but unconditional, self-giving love.
Certainty and spiritual self-confidence
will only make sinners despair;
compassion and self-offering
will build them up and heal them.

I call you to follow my way, the way of the cross,
and when you have allowed my life
to fill you completely,
then I will draw the lost and the hopeless to me
through your hands and your words.

I have appointed you shepherd and star;
the star will give hope to those in darkness,
and guidance to those who are lost,
and the shepherd will feed and protect my people.
        Come, follow me.

— *Richard Hobbs*

O HAPPY FAULT

This is part of the Service of Light that heralds Easter Day:

This is the night when Jesus Christ
broke the chains of death
and rose triumphant from the grave.

What good would life have been to us,
had Christ not come as our Redeemer?

Father, how wonderful your care for us!
How boundless your merciful love!

To ransom a slave
you gave away your Son.

O happy fault, O necessary sin of Adam,
which gained for us so great a Redeemer!

Most blessed of all nights, chosen by God
to see Christ rising from the dead!

The power of this holy night
dispels all evil, washes guilt away,
restores lost innocence, brings mourners joy;
it casts out hatred, brings peace, and humbles earthly
pride.

Night truly blessed when Heaven is wedded to earth
and man is reconciled with God!

Therefore, heavenly Father, in the joy of this night,
receive our ... sacrifices of praise.

— *The Sunday Missal, p. 211*

HALLELUJAH! HE IS RISEN

Each year, here in Cyprus, my husband and I lead an Easter Retreat. It begins with a celebration of the Last Supper on Maundy Thursday evening and ends on Easter Monday. Most of the meetings take place outside – in the olive groves or beside a cave that is reminiscent of the garden tomb. On Easter Sunday morning, while it is still dark, we walk to this tomb and wait in silence for the sun to rise. The silence is occasionally punctuated with music played on a portable cassette. At sunrise, there on the hillside overlooking the sea, we worship the Risen Lord. The following prayer came from a thankful heart one Easter Sunday morning.

> I saw you in the fullness of the moon
>   that lighted my path
>   on the way to the tomb.
> I saw you in the dove-shaped cloud
>   that hovered over the hills
>   as we waited for sunrise.
> I saw you in the sun which
>   slid over the mountain
>   in all its majesty
>   thrilling us with its appearance.
>
> I saw you in the liquid gold cross
>   traced on the sea
>   by the rays of the rising sun.
>
> I worshipped you
>   in the strains of the aria from Handel's Messiah
>   that heralded the sunrise:
>   'I know that my Redeemer liveth ...'
>
> I heard and felt you when,
>   like the angel,
>   I sat outside the Garden tomb
>   and wanted to shriek:
>   'He is not here ... he is risen.'
>
> Joy.
> Pure joy.   –   LJH

AUTUMN GLORY

On two occasions I have celebrated Easter in New Zealand when, of
course, it is autumn and not spring. On both occasions I have missed the
spring images and fumbled to find images that are married to the season.
Here Linnet has done just that and I am helped by it.

Liquid amber
foliage flaming
in sunkist splendour,
glorious extravagance
amid evergreen security,
magnificent
in dying –
at Easter.

Eternal Lord,
you shed your life
like autumn leaves
blood-red falling
from the tree,
lovelit to the end,
a nimbus of glory
against the darkest night,
majestic in your dying –
that Easter.

You are the Vine,
I, a branch,
as you are, I must be.
You blazed the way
to life through death.
I want to follow you,
to drop my finite foliage
too, in radiance
of self-giving love.
Saviour, I pray,
put your glory on display
in my dying –
this Easter, and always.

— *Linnet Hinton*

ON RETREAT

More and more people are discovering the value of Quiet Days and Retreats where we can step off the treadmill for a few hours, engage in some spiritual stock-taking and re-focus by fixing our gaze on God. The prayers that follow have been written during such times of stillness though this short section starts with a plea from God.

THE ONE VITAL THING

See communion with Myself as your *highest activity* ... there are no places on earth where this activity is impossible ...

Temptations to restrict the activity of communion with Me are often disguised as 'pressing duty', often involve misuse of time which will contribute nothing to your progress.

My child, *treasure* time spent, consciously, with Me, as I supply need for the hours ahead. Such communion, far from mere escaping, is *dynamic* in its essence ... and is indispensable for you. You were not meant to live without My resources.

Only one thing is vital ... (Luke 10:24).

– *John Woolley* [6]

RENEWAL

I came to you –
frightened, broken, naked –
ashamed and lonely!
You were to me –
a haven of refuge,
a deep gentle spring
of refreshing hope,
a gentle rain,
washing away dusty fears,
a warm summer sun
calling forth NEW LIFE!
Always –
a Guiding Light.

– *Isabel Radnett* [7]

NOTICING

This was written on a residential retreat:

'Too busy to be here?'
Too busy to be!
To rest and enjoy this:
I in you, you in me.
Too busy to wonder,
wander, just you and me.

My pace becomes slower,
the child starts to show.
What do trees feel like?
How do things grow?
I wander, I wonder,
what truths will he show?

The first day, I see it –
its occupant gone.
The form is near perfect,
but being moves on.
That place that is broken
has birthed a new song.

Cicada's wings – so fragile,
unseen by its eyes;
yet trusting its maker,
it unfolds them, and flies!
Things revealed to the infant
are hid from the wise.

Can *I* trust you, Lord?
Step forth from *my* shell?
Beat heart's wings I can't see?
To go where? I can't tell.
Your love, it allures me,
With words that compel:

'Come to me, learn of me,
I do all things well.'

– *David Crawley*

BURNED OUT

I prayed among the pine trees in the Troodos Mountains as I meditated on the verse: 'Jesus Christ laid down his life for us. And we ought to lay down our lives for our brothers' (1 John 3:16).

The burned-out pine tree draws me
    as a magnet draws iron filings.
I gaze long and hard at its woundedness:
    at the resin dangling from it,
       at the sun highlighting
           its richness and its redness.
I feel the breeze broadcasting the fragrance
    of its perfume.

I marvel that the tree has not only survived:
    it thrives,
       towering in all its splendour
          above the great gash caused by a streak
          of lightning.
'It's possible to be burned out
    yet to live'
       the scene whispers.

A nearby tree now beckons me.
    On its slender trunk
       I see a figure hanging:
          not desolate
            but triumphant.
              The Crucified.
My heart leaps for joy.
I am no longer alone
but one with you.

You give me your perspective.
    You lure me into the gash in the pine tree's side.
    You show me that there
       I can shelter from the wind.

May my wounds, Beloved,
        provide shelter
                for your hurting ones
                        today and always.

                    - LJH

LOVE REKINDLED

This was also written during a time of quiet in the Troodos Mountains.

I'm sitting in the forest
    hurting,
                burdened,
                        questioning.
Two great tits come to visit.
They hop on to the branch of the great pine
    under whose branches
                I'm sheltering from the sun.
                    They sit.
                            They sing.
                                They disappear.
'I know when one such fledgling falls,'
    you whisper.
            'And you are more precious to me
                than the smallest sparrow.'

I marvel.
    You know me through and through,
            yet I matter to you.
I transfer to you afresh
    the burden of my unanswered questions
            and my love for you is rekindled.

Thank you.

                    - LJH

HOMECOMING

This verse was written while praying with Frank Wesley's famous picture of the Prodigal. In this picture, the Indian artist has painted the Prodigal in such a way that it is clear that, unless the father holds on to him, he will keel over. I found this imagery consoling on this as on other occasions.

Father,
as I gazed at that picture of the prodigal
clasped in your arms,
feelings of relief swept over me.
I know it's where I am;
I know it's where I need to be.
I've given so much,
experienced so much.
Now, I just need to rest
in that place of true, undemanding homecoming,
in the safety and security
of your tender heart.

No words are needed.
I can collapse
and nestle
and be.

– *LJH*

Father,
may your love so spring up within me
that it overflows from me continually.
Remind me that if the source is clogged up
I have nothing to give.
Of myself I am nothing.

– *LJH*

GUNSHOTS

Twice a week in 'the hunting season', men dressed in army gear scour and scar the beautiful countryside that surrounds my home hunting for birds which they shoot and then pickle. As often happens, on one of my Quiet Days, gunshots coincided with the sound of the church bells that called the villagers to worship. The bells remind us that we are being prayed for by the village priest. These twin sounds – the shots and the church bells– made a profound impact on me, as they often do. I thought of the birds that would be left maimed, half dead, flapping injured wings that had lost their ability to fly. And I thought of villagers who would be consoled by God in the precincts of the church. This prayer rose from somewhere inside me.

> Keep me, O Lord,
> from slaughtering others
> with the witch-hunt of my gossip,
>   with the gunshots of my tongue,
>   with the cruelty of neglect.

> Rather, make of my heart
>   a holy home where
>   people can come,
>   find consolation,
>   peace
>   and YOU.

> – *LJH*

MAGNIFY THE LORD WITH ME

O most high,
    glorious God,
        how great is my dilemma!
In your aweful presence
    silence seems best.
And yet, if I keep my peace,
    the rocks themselves will cry out.
Yet if I speak, what will I say?

It is Love that calls forth my speech,
    though it feels like stammering.
        I love you, Lord God.
           I adore you.
               I bow down before you.
I thank you for your gifts of grace:
    the consistency of sunrise and sunset,
    the wonder of colours,
    the solace of voices I know.
I magnify you, Lord.
    Let me see your greatness –
    let me receive it.
    Help me bow in your presence
        in endless wonder
           and ceaseless praise.
In the name of him whose adoration never failed.

>   – *Slight adaptation of*
>   *Richard Foster's prayer* [8]

Enjoying God's World

'Creation can become a prime source of dialogue with Jesus as we seek to grow in our love relationship with him ...'

All creation bears the traces of God and will lead the spiritually sensitive observer back to the Trinity through Christ ...

If we look and listen with the eyes and ears of faith, all creation will 'declare the glory of God' (Ps. 19:1), which is in Jesus Christ, the divine Word of the Trinity.[1]

> Whoever is not enlightened by such brilliance of things created
>   must be blind;
> whoever is not awakened by their mighty voice must be deaf;
> whoever fails to praise God for all His works must be dumb;
> whoever fails to discover the First Principle through these signs
>   must be a fool.[2]

I believe these truths passionately. I teach them to others and delight to suggest ways in which would-be people of prayer can discover such truths for themselves. One day I was sitting on a deserted beach, fingering the multicoloured miniature stones that line the shore, basking in the warmth of the setting sun, relishing the song of the sea and expecting God to speak through these signs of his craftsmanship. But God seemed to be strangely silent that day.

Pondering the mystery of the seeming silence, I wandered along 'my' beach, the place where I go most days to pray. And I continued along my hour-long prayer walk. This walk takes me off the beach, through orange groves and past vineyards to the brow of a hill that affords a panoramic view of one of the most idyllic parts of the island of Cyprus. As though I was seeing this breath-taking view for the very first time, I stopped to stand and stare at the medley of colours above and below me: the slate blue of the sky merging with the azure blue of the sea, the silver-green of the olive trees mottled with the ambers and golds of the walnut leaves and the browns and bronzes of the vines. As I marvelled at this harmony, I listened to Vespers being chanted by the birds. 'What are you saying to me through the mysteries before me?' I whispered to God. Clear as a bell, three words popped into my mind.

'Just enjoy them.' I laughed. And I obeyed. Consequently, I returned home, no longer tense or intense but renewed in body, mind and spirit.

'Just enjoy them.' Those words still influence me. I find them curiously liberating. They help me to grasp the fact that God doesn't want us to become over-intense in our relationship with him. He wants us to relax and to find joy in his renewing and renewable gifts.

A few days later, I looked on my bookshelves for books on joy. There were volumes on grief and depression, spiritual warfare and marriage problems, loneliness, conflict, and the forgiveness of sins – but none on joy. I know that I have two books on the subject in England but they are not on my shelves here in Cyprus. One is *Joy* by Louis Evely. As I explained in *Listening to Others,* this Jesuit priest claims that the inability to receive joy is a universal problem; that though Jesus made us depositaries of his joy and though Christianity is a religion of joy, Christians somehow seem to have missed their entry into joy's fullness. We are better disposed to be sorrowful with Christ and to share his sufferings than to become participators in Resurrection joy.

I turned to Genesis 1 where we read that, on the sixth day, having created the world, 'God saw all that he had made, and it was very good.'

> God resting;
> God relishing;
> God marvelling
> at the mysteries he had made.
> God savouring;
> God enjoying;
> God embracing
> the wonders
> his Creator-hands had crafted.

My mind went to the poet Gerard Manley Hopkins. Surely, here is someone who discovered the secret of enjoying, savouring, relishing, marvelling, embracing God's world? Was not that the reason he could write memorable lines like these:

> The world is charged with the grandeur of God.
> It will flame out, like shining from shook foil ... [3]

and

> Nothing is so beautiful as spring –
>> When weeds, in wheels, shoot long and lovely and lush ...
>> The glassy pear tree leaves and blooms, they brush
>> The descending blue; that blue is all in a rush
> With richness; the racing lambs too have fair their fling.
> What is all this juice and all this joy?
>> A strain of the earth's sweet being in the beginning
> In Eden garden. [4]

and

> Glory be to God for dappled things –
> For skies of couple-colour as a brinded cow
> For rose-moles all in stipple upon trout that swim ... [5]

The prayers in this section start with the plea that we may learn to find God everywhere. They continue with unashamed expressions of enjoyment of the wonders of God's world.

GOD WITHIN, GOD EVERYWHERE

This prayer, written in 1514, is as relevant today as on the day it was penned.

> God be in my head,
> > and in my understanding;
> God be in my eyes,
> > and in my looking;
> God be in my mouth,
> > and in my speaking;
> God be in my heart,
> > and in my thinking;
> God be at my end,
> > and at my departing.

IN PRAISE OF CREATION

> Lord, may we love
> > and respect
> > > all your creation,
> all the earth
> > and every grain of sand in it.
> May we love every leaf,
> > and every ray of light.

> – *F. Dostoevsky* [6]

THE CREATOR

Almighty Creator, you who made all things:
the world cannot express all your glories,
even though the grass and the trees should sing.
You have wrought such a multitude of wonders
that they cannot be equalled or expressed.
So it is not hard work to praise you, Holy Trinity
nor to praise you, Son of Mary.

> – *LJH: adaptation of
> an early Welsh poem*

JOY

As the hand is made for holding
and the eye for seeing,
you have fashioned me, O Lord,
for joy
Share with me the vision
to find that joy everywhere:
in the wild violet's beauty,
in the lark's melody,
in the face of a compassionate person,
in a child's smile,
in the love of parents,
in the purity of Jesus.

> – *LJH: adaptation of
> a Celtic prayer*

I PRAISE YOU

For setting me free
    to delight in
        donkeys and trees,
            sun and moon,
                sky and stars,
                    extravagant colours
                        and miniature wild flowers
I praise you, O God.

For begging me to enjoy
    the filigree-fragrance of the almond blossom,
        the blues and turquoises of the sea,
           starlike grasses
              and open-faced anemones
I praise you, dear Lord.

For prompting me to chuckle
    at the antics of ducks,
        and monkeys,
           of turtles
              and striped fish,
I praise you, Creator God.

For the sheer enjoyment of your world
I give you thanks.

                                – LJH

THANK YOU, LORD

For all the first sweet flushings of the spring;
the greening earth, the tender heavenly blue;
the rich brown furrows gaping for the seed;
for all thy grace in bursting bud and leaf ...
for hedgerows sweet with hawthorn and wild rose;
for meadows spread with gold and gemmed with stars,
for every tint of every tiniest flower,
for every daisy smiling in the sun;
for every bird that builds in joyous hope,
for every lamb that frisks beside its dam,
for every leaf that rustles in the wind,
for spiring poplar, and for spreading oak,
for queenly birch, and lofty swaying elm;
for the great cedar's benedictory grace,
for earth's ten thousand fragrant incenses,
sweet altar-gifts from leaf and fruit and flower ...
for ripening summer and the harvesting;
for all the rich autumnal glories spread –
the flaming pageant of the ripening woods,
the fiery gorse, the heather purpled hills,
the rustling leaves that fly before the wind
and lie below the hedgerows whispering;
for meadows silver-white with hoary dew;
for sheer delight of tasting once again
that first crisp breath, of winter in the air;
the pictured pane; the new white world without;
the sparkling hedgerows' witchery of lace,
the soft white flakes that fold the sleeping earth;
the cold without, the cheerier warmth within ...
for all the glowing heart of Christmastide,
we thank thee, Lord!

– *John Oxenham* [7]

A COUNTRY WALK

I walked today, Lord,
such a glorious walk:
      sparkling air,
           fresh sea breeze,
                clear blue sky,
                      uninterrupted sunshine.

'Look at the birds,' you insisted,
I did.
They chattered
      they soared
           they swooped
                and some paused
                    to drink from the puddles
                        formed by last night's rain.

'Contemplate the lilies,' you whispered.
I did.
At a carpet of purple, pink and cream anemones.
Oh! And I picked blackberries,
found three big pine cones that begged to decorate our home for
Christmas,
collected windfalls – juicy mandarin oranges
then came back to bake bread.
While kneading the dough,
through the kitchen window I spied
      a huge cheese-shaped moon peeping over the mountain range.
'My gift,' you seemed to say
'to remind you that I love you.'

Joy.
Tears of joy.
True contentment.

                – *LJH*

HIS VOICE

His voice, never silent,
rolls along the shore,
surges across the sands,
echoes off cliffs,
thunders over falls,
roars down mountainsides,
drum-beats drought-taut ground –
in continuous communication
with creation,
a vibrant cascade
of life-giving sound.
It sings in my veins,
throbs in my heart,
stirs my stagnant spirit
to a crescendo of desire.
I drink it in deeply
yet thirst for more,
unsatisfied until at last
my calloused ears can hear
beyond fluid sound
the solid shape of words.

– *Linnet Hinton* [8]

'And his voice was like the sound of many waters.'

THE BEACH

Great waves, crashing, foaming,
   running up the sand.
To stop gently at its edge.
   Wonder!

– *M. Chanel O'Donnell,*
New Zealand

SUNRISE

I wrote this on the rooftop of the guest house where we were staying in
Pokhara, Nepal. The owner of the guest house had hammered on our door
to alert us to the fact that there would be a stunning sunrise that day. The
rooftop afforded a spectacular view of Nepal's famed Annapurna range of
mountains: Annapurna One, Two and Three and the Fishtail mountain –
once seen, never forgotten.

The marvels of your creation bring me
     endless delight, dear Lord:
  the crescent moon,
  the one, solitary star shining so steadfastly
    from the grey-blue sky,
  the chatter of the birds,
  the majesty of the mountains,
  the glow of the sky,
  and the shafts of light that signal
      the sun's rising.

The glow is subsiding,
the sky turning the colour of opals,
clouds enshroud the mountains.
They tell me you are holy
and remind me of your Shekinah glory.
One puffy cloud turns from grey to pink.
Now another,
   now another,
yet the sun is nowhere to be seen
so the mountains remain a solid black mass.

Breathless with wonder
  I wait and watch.
The clouds, now purply-pink, disperse.
The unseen sun tinges
   first the peak of the Fishtail Mountain,
   now the crest of Annapurna One.
The pink is spreading from the Fishtail's tip
   right down its giant sides
     and Annapurna Three begins to glint in the glory.

Annapurna One is now ablaze
  and birdsong fills the air:
  crows cawing,
  a sparrow chirping,
  the tree-top choir carolling
while Annapurna Two reflects the sun's light.

At last, the sun, a resplendent red ball,
slides slowly and surreptitiously over the tree-tops
where it hangs like a silent balloon –
further transforming the mountain-tops
  from starkness to softness,
  from grimness to glory.

The ever-changing spectacle
banishes yesterday's deep-down weariness.
I feel refreshed
simply by responding to your invitation
to enjoy your wonderful world.

       – LJH

RAINDROPS

 Raindrops dangling
   like bright baubles
     on the fronds of the bottle-brush tree.
 Enjoy them.

      – LJH

SUNSET

One part of the sky
seemed like a frothing, foaming sea tonight, Lord,
not white suds
but swirls of pink
tinged with purple.
And across the steel blue of a cloudless patch of sky
someone seemed to be stretching streamers –
fluorescent pink that changed before my eyes
from flamingo to vermilion to purple.
Cars rushed by –
occupants oblivious of the pageant in the sky.
But I stood riveted,
awed,
transfixed by the grandeur.
Was it colour like this that prompted the Psalmist to
sing:
'The heavens declare the glory of God'?
As now, so then, did you throw open
the casements of heaven and allow him to gaze on
your beauty,
your majesty,
your magnificence,
your splendour?
Who can tell?
For beckoning me from my desk
and thrilling me afresh with this glimpse of your glory,
I give you humble and heartfelt thanks.

– *LJH*

SUNDOWN

This prayer was written at 2.30 one morning. I woke and lay in bed over-whelmed by the love of God. Into his love, I lifted those dearest to me; and I felt at peace. The image that flooded my mind was of the setting sun shim-mering on the sea near my home. My mind went to Jesus's injunction, 'When you pray say, "Father".' I went into my study to write. As I finished writing the prayer, my eyes lighted on a photograph on the wall – of a friend of mine cuddling his baby. The child is nestling his head into his fa-ther's neck and the father has his arms wrapped around his son. He is enfolding him in love, gazing at him adoringly. They are, indeed, two yet one.

Father,
as the soon-setting sun
pours its rays on to the shimmering sea,
      warming it,
           transforming it,
so you beam the radiance of your life-giving love
on to me,
      into me,
consoling me,
transforming me.

For the wonder of this undeserved,
           unconditional,
                healing love

I praise you.
I bask in it,
      absorb it,
           relish it,
              abandon myself to it,
                delight in it;
I plumb its depths
      and begin to understand the mystery:
        I am in you
          and you are in me.
We are separate,
        different,
yet gloriously one.

          – *LJH*

A SACRIFICE OF PRAISE

For the beauty of the earth,
for the beauty of the skies,
for the love which from our birth
over and around us lies,
Christ our God, to you we raise
this our sacrifice of praise.

For the beauty of each hour
of the day and of the night,
hill and vale, and tree and flower,
sun and moon and stars of light.
Christ our God, to you we raise
this our sacrifice of praise.

For the joy of ear and eye,
for the heart and mind's delight,
for the mystic harmony
linking sense to sound and sight.
Christ our God, to you we raise
this our sacrifice of praise.

For the joy of human love,
brother, sister, parent, child,
friends on earth and friends above,
pleasures pure and undefiled,
Christ our God, to you we raise
this our sacrifice of praise.

For each perfect gift divine
to our race so freely given
joys bestowed by love's design
flowers of earth and fruits of heaven,
Christ our God, to you we raise
this our sacrifice of praise.

— F. S. Pierpoint (1835–1917)

SAVOURING SOUNDS

The soughing of the wind.
The roaring of the sea.
The rustling of the leaves of the walnut trees.
The carolling of the birds.
The scrunch, scrunch, scrunch of my lone footsteps.
I'm enjoying to the full,
Lord God,
your mysterious gift of hearing.

– *LJH*

THANK YOU

Goats grazing,
     sun setting,
         wagtails paddling,
             wild-flowers beckoning,
               birds chattering,
and the first white almond-blossom peeping
    from a tree that looks oh! so dead.

Thank you.

– *LJH*

WAS IT YOU?

Someone smudged the sky with pink
    this morning, Lord.
Was it you?

Someone even painted the sea pink.
Was that you?

No camera could capture
    the mystery,
        the majesty,
            the magic
of those flamingo pink
    smears and smudges and streaks
        mingling with the cloudless blue
            of a winter's sky.
No paint-brush could colour the sea
    salmon pink.
It must have been you.

Someone filled the air
    with bird-song this morning, Lord.
Was it you?
Did you set the cockerels crowing,
    the robins warbling,
        the sparrows twittering,
            the great tits singing 'pink-pink', 'see-saw'.
No human visionary could dream up the dawn chorus.
It must have been you.

                – *LJH*

ENGLAND IN SEPTEMBER

When people have served God overseas for even a short while, one of the problems they face on their return to the homeland is 'reverse culture shock', that is the shock of being suddenly confronted with what once was familiar but which now appears strange, even alien. In September 1995, I made a brief stop-over in England and wondered how I would find it. I wrote the following as a result of travelling through Kent by train – thrilled at the beginning of autumn.

> For
> sparkling air and
> scarlet berries;
> contemplative cows
> and luscious grass;
> oak leaves
> and acorns,
> silver birch trees
> and golden leaves,
> friendly train guards
> and silent companions,
> for this faint familiarity
> resurrecting a glut of happy memories
> I give you thanks
> O God.
>
> For the ease of re-rooting,
> for these simple pleasures,
> for the sense of security
> and joy of belonging,
> I praise you from the very depths
> of my being.
>
> – *LJH*

SIMPLE PLEASURES

I picked blackberries today, Lord,
not plump, juicy ones like I'd pick in England
but blackberries just the same –
enough to stew with apples for supper.
I collected mandarin oranges, too –
windfalls lying beneath trees
laden with fruit that looks so much like
    lights adorning the branches.
Oh! And I saw a robin:
red-breasted,
open-beaked,
singing full throttle
in the corner of the garden
it frequented last year.
Such simple pleasures.
Were these the mysteries
you surveyed
on that first Sabbath day
when you stopped and stared and confessed:
'It's good'?

– *LJH*

THE BEAUTY OF GOD

Ah, Lord God,
if the things you have made are so wonderful,
how exceedingly beautiful and ravishing
you must be in yourself.

– *LJH: adaptation of a prayer of*
Blessed Henry Suso (1300–66)

RIOTOUS COLOUR

The russets of the vineyards,
the scarlets of the poinsettias,
the purples of the bougainvilleas,
the pinks of the geraniums;
thank you, God, for riotous colour.

The soft-silver of the olive trees,
the muted mauve of the grape hyacinths,
the speedwell-blue of the sky,
soil the colour of coffee;
thank you, God, for quiet colours.

The greens and lemons of the variegated ivies,
the yellows and browns of the bronzing pomegranate trees,
the purples and pinks of a speckled sky at sunset,
the rainbow of colours created by corals;
thank you, God, for mottled colours.

The wispy-whiteness of the clouds,
the sapphire-blueness of the sea,
the virgin greenness of the meadows,
the sleek-brownness of the sheep and the goats.

Thank you, God, for creating colours –
    colours that dazzle,
        colours that soothe,
            colours that move,
                colours that harmonise,
                    colours that fill endless hours
                        with sheer delight.

– *LJH*

THANK YOU FOR THE NIGHT

Lord, I thank you for the night,
the time of cool and quiet,
the time of sweet enchantment
when a deep mystery pervades everything.
The time when soul speaks to soul in common desire
to partake of the hush of the ineffable.
The time when the moon and the stars
speak to man of his high calling and destiny.
The time of repose and calm
when the fever of the mind subsides
and uncertainty gives place
to the sense of eternal purpose.
O Lord, I thank you for night.

> – *LJH: adaptation of*
> *Chandran Devansen's prayer*
> *from India* [9]

O Lord, our Lord,
how majestic is your name in all
 the earth!
You have set your glory above
 the heavens ...
When I consider your heavens,
 the work of your fingers,
the moon and the stars, which
 you have set in place,
[I ask] what is man that you are
 mindful of him?

> – *Psalm 8:1, 3, 4*

AOTEAROA* — MY HOMELAND

Aotearoa –
        my homeland so beautiful,
                freshness and greenness
                        restoring to wholeness.

Rock pools and seascapes
        shimmering
                glimmering
                        sunlight a-filtering.

Sky and sea oneness
        stretching beyond us,
                infinity breathless.
Seagulls a-crying,
        dipping and diving
                curving and gliding
                        in graceful air-riding …

Bush walks abundant,
        ferns, mosses and creepers,
                silence and stillness
                        peace deep within us.

Waterfall, cascades, streams
        babbling in chorus –
Breakers, foam surges,
        white fountains enormous.

Bird songs resounding
        trilling and thrilling,
                heartstirring, joyous,
                        spellbinding, rapturous.

I look at the sun as its rays pierce my being,
        up, upwards it draws me,
                it beckons so strongly,
                      up, upwards in spirit
                              to the warmth and true brightness,

SUN, SONSHIP within me
        embracing, dissolving,
                dancing in oneness
                        to tunes ever timeless.

O praise to You, SON, CREATOR, and SPIRIT,
        breathing forth beauty in all things around us,
                renewing, restoring, enhancing, creating,
I praise You and thank You for my homeland so bounteous.

                            − *Moira Ross*

*Aotearoa is the name for New Zealand

GLORY

Leaden sky,
        steel-grey sea,
                a great tit
                        swinging on the bottle-brush tree
and your sign of promise, Lord
        arching right across the valley:
                a double rainbow.
                        Glory!

                    − *LJH*

GODSONG

I heard your melody
in water, air and earth,
sung gently in clear flowing
stream and whispered
on the summer breeze,
with the swelling largo
of the sweet-smelling earth
as it nurtures spring growth
and mellows autumn fruitfulness.
In the call of the tui
and the bellbird,
in the shrilling of the
seagulls whirling over beach and bach★
and in the lamb's bleating cry
for its mother's milk,
in the counterpoint
of sun and shadow,
of calm and storm,
I recognised the myriad patterns
of your song in
all creating
and heard
it all as
Godsong.

– *Joan Parker*

★A 'bach' is the Kiwi word for a holiday home.

DREAMING

How sweet
to sit
alone
and dream
in peace,
of this
and that.
Of trees,
the rain,
bright light,
cool streams,
the wind,
birds' songs,
the sun.
To see
in mind
the waves
that curl
and break
on sands,
near cliffs.
To speak
to God
of joy
and love,
of life,
his Son,
our hopes.
To watch
a Maid
beside
her Babe
asleep
upon
the hay.

To think
and dwell

on joys
we've had
and friends
we loved
so well.
To close
the door
and still
the noise
and be
alone
with God.

– M. Marcella Roache

NATURE PRAYER

You paint the sunrises and sunsets.
You are the songwriter and conductor of the birds.
You are the one who sends the water for the clouds,
    rivers and earth.
You shape the mountains and arrange the stars
    in the sky.
You are the lifegiver and midwife
    for the animals of the fields.
You shape me and mould me and I thank you.
Never let me forget or neglect you.
Let me always respond to your thirst
    for my love.
And even when I feel worthless …
You be the power of love,
    the force of your Spirit within
    – loving you as you deserve to be loved
    – thanking you and praising you.

– Cathy

THE COBWEB

I slept; yet in the dewy night
The spider spun on.
Weaving a thread of silver
Into a web so fine.

Sometimes patching up
where the wind had come to tease.
Welcoming the dew-drops
to hang as silver beads.
                Wonder!

            – *Chanel O'Donnell*

Give us this day our daily discovery

            – *Dr Rendell Harris, Quaker* [10]

Bibliography

A New Zealand Prayer Book

Appleton, G., *The Oxford Book of Prayers* (OUP, 1985). By permission of Oxford University Press.

Askew, E., *A Silence and a Shouting* (The Leprosy Mission International).

Bergan, J. S. and Schwan, S. M., *Love: A Guide to Prayer* (St Mary's Press, 1985).

Cameron, B., *My Peruvian Journey* (RNDM Poetry).

Carden, J., *Another Day: Prayers of the Human Family* (Triangle, 1986).

Carden, J., *Empty Shoes* (Highway Press, no date).

Castle, T,. *A Treasury of Prayer* (Hodder and Stoughton, 1986).

'Dennis', in *Children's Letters to God*.

Elliott, C., *Praying the Kingdom* (Darton, Longman & Todd).

Fleming, D.L., *The Spiritual Exercises of St Ignatius* (Institute of Jesuit Sources, 1978).

Foster, R., *Prayer* (Hodder and Stoughton, 1992).

Hinton, L., *Keep Me Singing: Songs of Pilgrimage* (Bible College of Victoria, no date).

Hudson, T., *Christ-following* (Hodder and Stoughton, 1996).

Hutson, J., *Heal My Heart, O Lord* (Ave Maria Press, 1976).

Job, R.P. and Shawchurch, N., *A Guide to Prayer* (The Upper Room, USA, 1983).

Kidd, S.M., *Until the Heart Waits* (Harper and Row, 1990).

Lisbeth CHN (trans.), *Mary's Key: A Guided Walk with Mary Through Her Song of Praise* (Stiftelsen Vetekomet, Sweden, no date).

Mary, Mother & Ware, Archimandrite Kallistos, *The Lenten Triodion* (Faber & Faber, 1984).

Milner-White, E., *My God, My Glory* (SPCK, 1994).

Nouwen, H., *The Life of the Beloved* (Hodder and Stoughton, 1992).

Pelletier, M.E., *Embrace the World* (Sisters of the Good Shepherd, 1993).

Peterson, E.H., *Praying with the Psalms* (HarperCollins, 1993).

Pooley, R. and Seddon, P., *The Lord of the Journey* (Collins, 1986).

Puhl, Louis J., *The Spiritual Exercises of St Ignatius* (The Newman Press, 1951).

Rae, D., *Love Until it Hurts* (Hodder and Stoughton, 1981).

RNDM Poetry (unpublished collection of poems, no date).

Rohr, H., *Set Me Free* (Spectrum Publications, 1972).

Talbot, John Michael, *The Lover and the Beloved* (Marshall Pickering, 1985).

The Sunday Missal (Collins, 1977).

Vanier, J., *The Broken Body* (Darton, Longman & Todd, 1988).

Veltri, J., *Orientations* (Loyola House, Ontario, no date).

Ward, J. N., *Five for Sorrow, Ten for Joy* (Epworth).

Woolley, J., *I Am With You* (I Am With You Publishing, 1984).

Notes

Introduction

1. *Christ-following*, pp. 97 & 92.
2. *Embrace the World*, p. 69.
3. Ibid., p. 69.
4. Ibid., p. 45.
5. Ibid., p. 76.
6. Ibid., p. 76.

Enjoying Intimacy With God

1. *Mary's Key: A Guided Walk with Mary Through Her Song of Praise*.
2. *Love: A Guide to Prayer*, p. 11, with permission.
3. *I Am With You*, p. 10.
4. Ibid., p. 10.
5. *The Oxford Book of Prayers*, pp. 56–7, by permission of Oxford University Press.
6. *My God, My Glory* , p. 10.
7. *Embrace the World*, p. 69.
8. *Orientations*, p. 46.

Help Me To Say Yes

1. *The Life of the Beloved* , pp. 30–1.
2. *The Broken Body*, pp. 72–3.
3. *Heal My Heart, O Lord*, p. 38.
4. *RNDM Poetry*.
5. *Set Me Free*.
6. *The Spiritual Exercises of St Ignatius* .
7. *My Peruvian Journey*.
8. *Love Until It Hurts*.
9. *I Am With You*, p. 18.
10. *A Silence and a Shouting*.
11. *The Spiritual Exercises of St Ignatius* (Puhl).
12. *Embrace the World*, p. 8.
13. *RNDM Poetry*.

When Times Are Tough

1. *A Guide to Prayer*, p. 336.
2. *The Message*, pp. 15–16.
3. *I Am With You*.
4. Ibid., p. 26.
5. *Heal My Heart, O Lord*, pp. 30–1.
6. *I Am With You*, p. 5.
7. Ibid., p. 26.
8. *Until the Heart Waits*, p. 93.

9. *I Am With You,* p. 1.
10. *Heal My Heart, O Lord,* pp. 32–3.
11. *Praying With the Psalms.*
12. Previously unpublished prayer.

Going Where It Hurts
1. *The Message,* p. 63.
2. *Another Day: Prayers of the Human Family,* pp. 15, 16.
3. *Five for Sorrow, Ten for Joy.*
4. *Keep Me Singing: Songs of Pilgrimage,* p. 32.
5. Ibid., pp. 12–13.
6. *Empty Shoes,* p. 24.
7. Ibid., p. 27.
8. Ibid., pp. 44–5.
9. Ibid., pp. 56–7.
10. Ibid., pp. 80–1.
11. *Another Day,* pp. 65–6.

Serving In All Seasons
1. Last three lines from *My God, My Glory,* p. 16.
2. *The Sunday Missal,* p. 558.
3. *Children's Letters to God.*
4. *The Lord of the Journey,* p. 142.
5. *The Lenten Triodion,* p. 587.
6. *I Am With You,* p. 21.
7. *RNDM Poetry.*
8. *Prayer,* p. 96.

Enjoying God's World
1. *The Lover and the Beloved,* pp. 15–20.
2. Ibid., p. 20.
3. *Poems and Prose of Gerard Manley Hopkins,* p. 27.
4. Ibid., p. 28.
5. Ibid., p. 30.
6. From *The Brothers Karamazov* in *A Treasury of Prayer,* p. 82.
7. Ibid., p. 85.
8. *Keep Me Singing: Songs of Pilgrimage,* p. 33
9. *Another Day,* p. 330.
10. Ibid., p. 19.

Index of First Lines